D1466587

The
Wiersbe
BIBLE STUDY SERIES

The Wiersbe
BIBLE STUDY SERIES

LEVITICUS

Becoming

"Set Apart"

for God

David C Cook®
transforming lives together

THE WIERSBE BIBLE STUDY SERIES: LEVITICUS
Published by David C Cook
4050 Lee Vance View
Colorado Springs, CO 80918 U.S.A.

David C Cook Distribution Canada
55 Woodslee Avenue, Paris, Ontario, Canada N3L 3E5

David C Cook U.K., Kingsway Communications
Eastbourne, East Sussex BN23 6NT, England

The graphic circle C logo is a registered trademark of David C Cook.

All Scripture quotations in this study are taken from the Holy Bible, New
International Version®, NIV®. Copyright © 1973, 1984 by Biblica, Inc.™ Used by
permission of Zondervan. All rights reserved worldwide. www.zondervan.com.

In the *Be Holy* excerpts, unless otherwise noted, all Scripture quotations are taken from
the King James Version of the Bible. (Public Domain.) Scripture quotations marked
NIV are taken from the Holy Bible, New International Version®, NIV®. Copyright ©
1973, 1984 by Biblica, Inc.™ Used by permission of Zondervan. All rights reserved
worldwide. www.zondervan.com; and NKJV are taken from the New King James Version®.
Copyright © 1982 by Thomas Nelson, Inc. Used by permission. All rights reserved.

All excerpts taken from *Be Holy*, second edition, published by David C Cook
in 2010 © 1994 Warren W. Wiersbe, ISBN 978-1-4347-0053-7.

ISBN 978-1-4347-0696-6
eISBN 978-0-7814-1278-0

© 2015 Warren W. Wiersbe

The Team: Karen Lee-Thorp, Amy Konyndyk, Nick Lee, Jack Campbell, Karen Athen
Series Cover Design: John Hamilton Design
Cover Photo: iStockphoto

Printed in the United States of America
First Edition 2015

1 2 3 4 5 6 7 8 9 10

112414

Contents

Introduction to Leviticus

Salt and Light

Whatever else the professing Christian church may be known for today—great crowds, expensive buildings, big budgets, political clout—it's not distinguished for its holiness. Bible-believing evangelical Christians make up a sizable minority in the United States, and our presence isn't making much of an impact on society. The salt seems to have lost its saltiness, and the light is so well hidden that the marketplace is quite dark.

Holiness

Happiness, not holiness, is the chief pursuit of most people today, including many professed Christians. They want Jesus to solve their problems and carry their burdens, but they don't want Him to control their lives and change their character. It doesn't disturb them that eight times in the Bible God said to His people, "Be holy, for I am holy," *and He meant it.*

"He that sees the beauty of holiness, or true moral good," wrote Jonathan Edwards, "sees the greatest and most important thing in the world." My prayer is that the study and application of the spiritual principles in Leviticus will make us more like Jesus Christ and better able to impact this present evil world.

—*Warren W. Wiersbe*

How to Use This Study

This study is designed for both individual and small-group use. We've divided it into eight lessons—each references one or more chapters in Warren W. Wiersbe's commentary *Be Holy* (second edition, David C Cook, 2010). While reading *Be Holy* is not a prerequisite for going through this study, the additional insights and background Wiersbe offers can greatly enhance your study experience.

The **Getting Started** questions at the beginning of each lesson offer you an opportunity to record your first thoughts and reactions to the study text. This is an important step in the study process as those "first impressions" often include clues about what it is your heart is longing to discover.

The bulk of the study is found in the **Going Deeper** questions. These dive into the Bible text and, along with helpful excerpts from Wiersbe's commentary, help you examine not only the original context and meaning of the verses but also modern application.

Looking Inward narrows the focus down to your personal story. These intimate questions can be a bit uncomfortable at times, but don't shy away from honesty here. This is where you are asked to stand before the mirror of God's Word and look closely at what you see. It's the place to take a good look at yourself in light of the lesson and search for ways in which you can grow in faith.

Going Forward is the place where you can commit to paper those things you want or need to do in order to better live out the discoveries you made in the Looking Inward section. Don't skip or skim through this. Take the time to really consider what practical steps you might take to move closer to Christ. Then share your thoughts with a trusted friend who can act as an encourager and accountability partner.

Finally, there is a brief **Seeking Help** section to close the lesson. This is a reminder for you to invite God into your spiritual-growth process. If you choose to write out a prayer in this section, come back to it as you work through the lesson and continue to seek the Holy Spirit's guidance as you discover God's will for your life.

Tips for Small Groups

A small group is a dynamic thing. One week it might seem like a group of close-knit friends. The next it might seem more like a group of uncomfortable strangers. A small-group leader's role is to read these subtle changes and adjust the tone of the discussion accordingly.

Small groups need to be safe places for people to talk openly. It is through shared wrestling with difficult life issues that some of the greatest personal growth is discovered. But in order for the group to feel safe, participants need to know it's okay *not* to share sometimes. Always invite honest disclosure, but never force someone to speak if he or she isn't comfortable doing so. (A savvy leader will follow up later with a group member who isn't comfortable sharing in a group setting to see if a one-on-one discussion is more appropriate.)

Have volunteers take turns reading excerpts from Scripture or from the commentary. The more each person is involved even in the mundane tasks, the more they'll feel comfortable opening up in more meaningful ways.

The leader should watch the clock and keep the discussion moving. Sometimes there may be more Going Deeper questions than your group can cover in your available time. If you've had a fruitful discussion, it's okay to move on without finishing everything. And if you think the group is getting bogged down on a question or has taken off on a tangent, you can simply say, "Let's go on to question 5." Be sure to save at least ten to fifteen minutes for the Going Forward questions.

Finally, soak your group meetings in prayer—before you begin, during as needed, and always at the end of your time together.

Sacrifices
(LEVITICUS 1—7)

Before you begin ...
- *Pray for the Holy Spirit to reveal truth and wisdom as you go through this lesson.*
- *Read Leviticus 1—7. This lesson references chapters 1 and 2 in* Be Holy. *It will be helpful for you to have your Bible and a copy of the commentary available as you work through this lesson.*

Getting Started

From the Commentary

Contrary to what you may hear today in some sermons and popular religious songs, the emphasis in the Bible is on the *holiness of God* and not on the love of God. "Love is central in God," wrote American theologian Augustus H. Strong, "but holiness is central in love." God's love is a holy love, for the Bible states that "God is light" (1 John 1:5) as well as "God is love" (4:8, 16). Love without holiness would be a monstrous thing that could destroy

God's perfect law, while holiness without love would leave no hope for the lost sinner. Both are perfectly balanced in the divine nature and works of God.

—*Be Holy*, pages 16–17

1. What is holiness? Why does the Bible emphasize holiness over love? How do the two work together? How does today's church address holiness?

More to Consider: Our English word holy *comes from the Old English word* halig, *which means "to be whole, to be healthy." What health is to the body, holiness is to the inner person. The word Moses used for "holy" in Leviticus means "to be set apart." How do both of these definitions work together to help us understand holiness?*

2. Choose one verse or phrase from Leviticus 1—7 that stands out to you. This could be something you're intrigued by, something that makes you uncomfortable, something that puzzles you, something that resonates with you, or just something you want to examine further. Write that here.

Going Deeper

From the Commentary

The Jewish priesthood belonged only to the tribe of Levi. Levi, the founder of the tribe, was the third son of Jacob and Leah (Gen. 29:34; 35:23) and the father of Gershon, Kohath, and Merari (46:11). Since Kohath's son Amram was the father of Aaron, Moses, and Miriam (Num. 26:58–59), Aaron, Moses, and Miriam belonged to the tribe of Levi.

Aaron was the first high priest and his male descendants became priests, with the firstborn son in each generation inheriting the high priesthood. (Every priest was a Levite, but not every Levite was a priest.) The rest of the men in the tribe of Levi (the "Levites") were assigned to serve as assistants to the priests. The Levites were the substitutes for the firstborn males in Israel, all of whom had to be dedicated to the Lord (Ex. 13:1–16; Num. 3:12–13, 44–51). To facilitate their ministry, David eventually divided the thousands of Levites into twenty-four "courses" (1 Chron. 23:6).

The name *Leviticus* comes from *Levi* and means "pertaining to the Levites." Actually, the Levites are mentioned in only one verse in this book (Lev. 25:32); the regulations in Leviticus pertain primarily to the priests. Of course, as assistants to the priests, the Levites would have to know what the Lord wanted done in the ministry of His house.

—*Be Holy*, page 19

3. What was the benefit of having the priests (and their assistants) come from just one tribe? What does this tell us about God during Old Testament times? How does the New Testament story change the priesthood (Heb. 5:4–10; 1 Peter 2:5, 9)?

From the Commentary

God's purpose for Israel was that the nation be "a kingdom of priests and a holy nation" (Ex. 19:6 NKJV). Everything in the life of the Old Testament Jew was either "holy" (set apart for God's exclusive use) or "common," and the "common" things were either "clean" (the people could use them) or "unclean" (it was forbidden to use them). The Jews had to be careful to avoid what was unclean; otherwise, they would find themselves "cut off from the people" until they had gone through the proper ceremony to be made clean again.

The laws governing marriage, birth, diets, personal cleanliness, the quarantine of diseased persons, and the burial of the dead, while they certainly involved hygienic benefits to the nation, were all reminders that God's people couldn't live any way they pleased. Because they were God's chosen people, the Jews had to learn to put a difference "between holy and unholy, and between unclean and clean" (Lev. 10:10). They must not live like the godless nations around them.

—*Be Holy*, pages 20–21

4. Why was there such a distinction between "clean" and "unclean" for God's people in Moses' time? In what ways did this help set the people apart? In what ways did this set up the possibility for abuse of the law? Are there parallels to this practice in today's church? Explain.

From the Commentary

The burnt offering (Lev. 1:1–17; 6:8–13) was the basic sacrifice that expressed devotion and dedication to the Lord. When we surrender ourselves to the Lord, we put "all on the altar" (1:9) and hold back nothing. The New Testament parallel is Romans 12:1–2, where God's people are challenged to be living sacrifices, wholly yielded to the Lord.

The ritual of the offering was spelled out by the Lord and could not be varied. The sacrifice had to be a male animal from the herd (Lev. 1:3–10) or the flock (vv. 10–14), or it could be a bird (vv. 14–17) and the worshipper had to bring the sacrifice to the door of the tabernacle, where a fire was constantly burning on a brazen altar (6:13). The priest examined the sacrifice to make sure it was without blemish (22:20–24), for we must give our very best to the Lord (see Mal. 1:6–14). Jesus Christ was a sacrifice "without blemish and without spot" (1 Peter 1:19), who gave Himself in total dedication to God (John 10:17; Rom. 5:19; Heb. 10:10).

Except when birds were sacrificed, the offerer laid a hand on the sacrifice (Lev. 1:4), an action which symbolized two things: (1) the offerer's identification with the sacrifice and (2) the transfer of something to the sacrifice. In the case of the burnt offering, the offerer was saying, "Just as this animal is wholly given to God on the altar, so I wholly give myself to the Lord." With the sacrifices that involved the shedding of blood, the laying on of hands meant the worshipper was symbolically transferring sin and guilt to the animal who died in the place of the sinner. Even the burnt offering made atonement for the offerer (v. 4).

The offerer then killed the animal, and the priest caught the blood in a basin and sprinkled the blood on the sides of the altar (vv. 5, 11). The priest, not the offerer, killed the bird and its blood was drained out on the side of the altar, and its body burned in the fire on the altar (vv. 15–17). The dead body of the bull, lamb, or goat was dismembered, and the parts washed. Then all of it but the hide was laid in order on the wood and burned in the fire. The hide was given to the priest (7:8).

—*Be Holy*, pages 28–29

5. Describe the "transaction" that occurred at the altar. (See also Lev. 6:9–13.) What was the significance of the offering?

From the Commentary

> The drink offering (Num. 15:1–13) is mentioned in Leviticus 23:13, 18, and 37, but its "laws" are not explained there. Like the meal offering, the drink offering was presented after the animal sacrifices had been put on the altar and was a required part of the sacrifice (see Num. 29:6, 11, 18–19, and so on). "The fourth part of a hin of wine" (15:5) would be about a quart of liquid. Neither the offerer nor the priest drank the wine, because all of it was poured out on the altar. Note that the more expensive sacrifices required a larger amount of wine for the drink offering.
>
> —*Be Holy*, pages 31–32

6. The burnt offering, the meal offering, and the drink offering all represent dedication to God and commitment to Him and His work. What specifically might the pouring out of the wine symbolize? (See Ps. 22:14; Isa. 53:12.) How does this relate to the way Paul was poured out (Phil. 2:17)? How was Paul himself "poured out like a drink offering" (2 Tim. 4:6)?

From the Commentary

There are several distinctive features about the peace offering or fellowship offering that should be noted. For one thing, the offerer could bring a female animal, something not permitted for the other animal sacrifices. If the offering was not in fulfillment of a vow, the sacrifice could have some defects and still be accepted (Lev. 22:23). After all, it was basically going to be used as food for the priests and the offerer's family, and those defects wouldn't matter.

That leads to our third distinctive feature: the fellowship offering is the only offering that was shared with the worshippers. After the priest had completed the sacrifice, a large portion of the meat went to him; the rest went to the offerer, who could then enjoy a feast with his family and friends. Since the Jews didn't often slaughter their precious animals for meat, a dinner of beef or lamb would be a special occasion. At the dedication of the temple, Solomon sacrificed 142,000 peace offerings and the people feasted for two weeks (1 Kings 8:62–66).

—*Be Holy*, page 32

7. What made the fellowship offering unique? How was this a precursor to the role of fellowship in the church today? Why was the sharing aspect of this offering so important to God's people in the time of Leviticus? Why is it important today?

From the Commentary

The sin offering and the guilt (or trespass) offering were very much alike and were even governed by the same law (Lev. 7:1–10). Generally speaking, the guilt offering was for individual sins that affected people and property and for which restitution could be made, while the sin offering focused on some violation of the law that was done without deliberate intent. The trespass offering emphasized the *damage* done to others by the offender, while the sin offering emphasized the offender's *guilt* before God. The priest would examine the offender and determine which sacrifice was needed.

—*Be Holy*, page 34

8. Why would the sin offering and guilt offering be governed by the same law? How do we deal with sin toward God in today's church? How do we deal with trespass against others? Is the difference meaningful to today's Christians? Why or why not? It's noted that no sacrifices were made for deliberate sins. Why was this the case? How did Jesus' death and resurrection change this?

More to Consider: Note the repeated use of "unintentionally" (the King James Version has "through ignorance") in Leviticus 4:2, 13, 22, 27; and 5:15. Does this mean the sinners were ignorant of the law? Explain. Does ignorance cancel guilt? Why or why not? (See also Ps. 19:12 where David used the same root word.)

From the Commentary

The sin offering (Lev. 4:1—5:13; 6:24–30) had to be brought to the Lord no matter who the sinner was, and the higher the sinner's position in the nation, the more expensive the sacrifice.… If the high priest sinned, he had to bring a young bullock (Lev. 4:1–12). If the whole congregation sinned, they also had to bring a bullock (vv. 13–21). A ruler brought a male kid of the goats (vv. 22–26), while one of the "common people" ("a member of the community," NIV) brought a female kid of the goats or a female lamb (vv. 27–35). A poor person could bring two doves or pigeons, and a very poor person could bring a nonbloody sacrifice of fine flour (5:7–13).

Whatever animal was brought, the offender had to identify with the sacrifice by laying hands on it. When the whole nation sinned, it was the elders who did this (4:15), for as leaders, they were responsible before God to oversee the spiritual life of the people. The animal was slain, and the blood presented to God. In the case of the high priest and the nation, some of the blood was sprinkled before the veil and applied to the horns of the altar of incense in the holy place, and the rest was poured out at the base of the altar.

—*Be Holy*, pages 34–35

9. Why did the sin offering differ based on the person presenting it? What are some of the ways an entire congregation could sin? In what ways was this system an attempt to be fair to all people? In what ways might the system have been abused? How might this scaled-offering way of thinking have influenced the way some believers today think about sin and forgiveness?

From the Commentary

The trespass offering (Lev. 5:14—6:17; 7:1–10) was needed for two kinds of sins: sins against "the holy things of the Lord" (5:15) and against one's neighbor (6:1–7). The first category included offenses that involved sacrifices to God, vows, celebration of the special days, and so on, while examples of the second category are given in verses 2–3.

The ritual involved the sinner confessing the sin (Num. 5:7), restoring the property involved or its equivalent in money, paying a fine equivalent to 20 percent of the value of the damaged property, and sacrificing a ram to the Lord

(Lev. 5:15, 18). The priest valued the ram to make sure of its worth, lest the offender try to atone for his or her sins by giving the Lord something cheap. The restitution and fine were first given to the priest so he would know it was permissible to offer the sacrifice (6:6). If the offended party wasn't available to receive the property or money, then it could be paid to one of the relatives; if no relative was available, it remained with the priest (Num. 5:5–10).

—*Be Holy*, page 36

10. How does the trespass or guilt offering illustrate that it is a very costly thing for people to commit sin and for God to cleanse sin? How do our sins hurt God and others? Respond to the following statement: True repentance will always bring with it a desire for restitution.

Looking Inward

Take a moment to reflect on all that you've explored thus far in this study of Leviticus 1—7. Review your notes and answers and think about how each of these things matters in your life today.

Tips for Small Groups: To get the most out of this section, form pairs or trios and have group members take turns answering these questions. Be honest and as open as you can in this discussion, but most of all, be encouraging and supportive of others. Be sensitive to those who are going through particularly difficult times and don't press for people to speak if they're uncomfortable doing so.

11. What does holiness mean to you? What are some ways you pursue holiness? What are some things that get in the way of that pursuit?

12. How comfortable would you have been living as one of God's people in the time of Moses? Would you have appreciated the specific laws and regulations? Why or why not? How does the way you live today compare to what you might have experienced then?

13. Do you think the amount of sacrifice given to pay for a sin ought to have been based on position in society? What about that system appeals to you? What about it bothers you? How does Jesus' sacrifice on your behalf change that system?

Going Forward

14. Think of one or two things that you have learned that you'd like to work on in the coming week. Remember that this is all about quality, not quantity. It's better to work on one specific area of life and do it well than to work on many and do poorly (or to be so overwhelmed that you simply don't try).

Do you want to deal with something that impedes your progress toward holiness? Be specific. Go back through Leviticus 1—7 and put a star next to the phrase or verse that is most encouraging to you. Consider memorizing this verse.

Real-Life Application Ideas: This week, consider what it means to pursue holiness as you go through your daily routines. How does holiness affect the way you approach each day? The way you relate to your family, friends, and coworkers? Ask God to help you understand the practical steps toward living a holier life, and ask Him to give you the wisdom to choose those steps. Then, when the week is done, think back on how this focus on holiness influenced your choices.

Seeking Help

15. Write a prayer below (or simply pray one in silence), inviting God to work on your mind and heart in those areas you've noted in the Going Forward section. Be honest about your desires and fears.

Notes for Small Groups:

- *Look for ways to put into practice the things you wrote in the Going Forward section. Talk with other group members about your ideas and commit to being accountable to one another.*

- *During the coming week, ask the Holy Spirit to continue to reveal truth to you from what you've read and studied.*

- *Before you start the next lesson, read Leviticus 8—10. For more in-depth lesson preparation, read chapter 3, "A Kingdom of Priests," in* Be Holy.

Priests
(LEVITICUS 8—10)

Before you begin ...
- *Pray for the Holy Spirit to reveal truth and wisdom as you go through this lesson.*
- *Read Leviticus 8—10. This lesson references chapter 3 in* Be Holy. *It will be helpful for you to have your Bible and a copy of the commentary available as you work through this lesson.*

Getting Started

From the Commentary

Under the old covenant, God's people had a priesthood; under the new covenant, God's people are a "holy priesthood" and a "royal priesthood" (1 Peter 2:5, 9). Every believer in Jesus Christ can say with the apostle John: "To Him who loved us and washed us from our sins in His own blood, and has made us kings and priests to His God and

Father, to Him be glory and dominion, forever and ever"
(Rev. 1:5–6 NKJV).

—*Be Holy*, page 41

1. God's desire was that the entire nation of Israel be "a kingdom of priests and a holy nation" (Ex. 19:6). How well did they do in achieving that? (See Isa. 1:4.) How did the nation's sinfulness set the stage for God's law? For God's plan to send His Son, Jesus? Could there have been another way to prepare the people for God's grace? Explain.

2. Choose one verse or phrase from Leviticus 8—10 that stands out to you. This could be something you're intrigued by, something that makes you uncomfortable, something that puzzles you, something that resonates with you, or just something you want to examine further. Write that here.

Going Deeper

From the Commentary

> God wants His church today to be "a holy nation, a people belonging to God, that [they] may declare the praises of him who called [them] out of darkness into his wonderful light" (1 Peter 2:9 NIV). The Jewish priests were a privileged people, yet they despised their privileges and helped lead the nation into sin. Even after the Jews returned to their land from Babylon and established their worship again, the priests didn't give God their best, and God had to rebuke them (Mal. 1:6—2:17).
>
> —*Be Holy*, pages 41–42

3. How can today's church become a "holy nation"? What would that look like? How does the church as a holy nation fit into the world at large? How would this type of church relate to our secular government?

More to Consider: At least twenty times in Leviticus 8—10 you'll find the word "commanded," particularly in the phrase "as the LORD commanded Moses." God was very clear about the instructions He gave His people. How do church leaders today know what God commands them to do? What happens when we substitute people's ideas for God's commands? (See Isa. 8:20.)

From the Commentary

> In Leviticus 8:6, Aaron and his sons washed. This may have been done at the laver in the courtyard of the tabernacle (Ex. 38:8). The priests were ceremonially bathed all over but once; from then on, they washed their hands and feet at the laver while they were serving in the tabernacle (30:17–21). When sinners trust Christ, they are washed from their sins once and for all (Rev. 1:5–6; 1 Cor. 6:9–11); God's children need to keep their feet clean by confessing their sins to the Lord (John 13:1–10; 1 John 1:9).
>
> —*Be Holy*, page 43

4. Why is washing such a familiar theme in Scripture? (See also Ps. 119:9; John 15:3; Eph. 5:25–27.) What was the point of the ceremonial washing in Moses' time? What is its symbolic meaning today? How does the Word cleanse us and make us more like Christ?

From Today's World

In the ministry of today's church, spiritual leaders must constantly ask, "What does the Scripture say?" (Rom. 4:3). God hasn't left us in the dark as to what His church is, how it's to be led, and what it's supposed to do, but if we substitute people's ideas for God's Word, we *will* be in the dark (Isa. 8:20). Religious novelties and fads abound, creating celebrities and increasing crowds but not always honoring the Lord or building the church.

5. What are some of the religious fads and novelties in today's church? Why are they so popular? How do we determine the difference between an idea that serves people and an idea that serves and honors God when it comes to churches and church programs? Why is this important to the spiritual life of the church?

From the Commentary

In Leviticus 8:10–12, Moses anointed Aaron and the tabernacle. This was done with a special oil that no one was to duplicate in the camp, nor was it to be used on anyone but a priest (Ex. 30:22–33). In Scripture, oil is often a symbol of the Spirit of God who has anointed each believer (2 Cor. 1:21; 1 John 2:20, 27; see Ps. 133).

The Hebrew word *Messiah* and the Greek word *Christ* both mean "anointed one" (Luke 4:18; Acts 10:38).

—*Be Holy*, page 44

6. How did the anointing oil of the Lord set the priests apart from the common people? What were some of the things priests were disallowed from doing? Why was being set apart so important in this context? What does the symbol of anointing oil come to mean in the New Testament?

From the Commentary

Aaron and his sons had obeyed God's commandments. Thus when the week was over, they were ready to begin serving the Lord at the altar. Up to this point, Moses had been offering the sacrifices; now Aaron and his sons would take up their priestly ministry.

Aaron and his sons had to offer a bull calf for a sin offering and a ram for a burnt offering; from then on, they would be offering a burnt offering on the altar every morning and evening (Lev. 9:17; Ex. 29:38–42). Each day must begin and end with total consecration to the Lord. Being imperfect, the priests had to offer sacrifices for themselves first before they could offer sacrifices for the people (see Heb. 7:25–28).

Their ordination, however, also involved offering sacrifices for the people (Lev. 9:3–4): a goat for a sin offering, a calf and a lamb for burnt offerings, and a bullock and a ram for peace (fellowship) offerings, along with the meal offerings.

—*Be Holy*, pages 45–46

7. Review Leviticus 9:1–21. Why would it have been wrong to have sanctified priests without a sanctified people? How did the sacrifices made by the priests on behalf of the people sanctify them? How does Jesus do this for us today?

From the Commentary

One of the privileges of the high priest was that of blessing the people; on that first day of his ministry, Aaron gave them *two* blessings. He gave the first one alone, after he had offered the sacrifices; he gave the second one along with Moses after they had come out from the tabernacle when the ordination ceremony was finished.

The first blessing was probably the high priestly blessing recorded in Numbers 6:23–26. It followed the sacrifices.... The second blessing followed the time Moses and Aaron had in the tabernacle.

—*Be Holy*, pages 46–47

8. Read Numbers 6:23–26. What does it mean to have God "turn his face toward you" (v. 26)? Why is it a blessing when He does this? What is the purpose of a formal blessing like this? When is it appropriate to have blessings like this today?

From the Commentary

The glory of the Lord had appeared when Moses finished erecting the tabernacle (Ex. 40:33–35), and it would appear again at the dedication of the temple (2 Chron. 7:1ff.). How gracious on God's part to share His glory with sinful people!

The glory that dwelt in the tabernacle eventually left the camp because of the sins of the people (1 Sam. 4:21). It returned at the dedication of the temple, but then the prophet Ezekiel watched it depart because the nation had become so sinful (Ezek. 8:4; 9:3; 10:4, 18; 11:22–23). The glory came to earth when Jesus was born (Luke 2:8–9) and tabernacled in Him (John 1:14), but sinful people nailed that glory to a cross. Today, God's glory dwells in the bodies of His people (1 Cor. 6:19–20), in each local assembly of His people (3:16–17), and in His church collectively (Eph. 2:19–22). One day, we shall see that glory lighting the perfect heavenly city that God is preparing for His people (Rev. 21:22–23).

—*Be Holy*, page 47

9. Why did the people shout for joy in Leviticus 9:24? Why did they fall facedown? How does this paradoxical response help us better understand the experience of worship? How can celebration and fear go together? (See Ps. 2:11.) Read 1 Corinthians 14:23–25. What were Paul's thoughts about this experience in the local church?

More to Consider: In 2 Chronicles 7:1–3, the fire of God consumed the burnt offering and gave the people the assurance that Jehovah God was among them and with them. "Our God is a consuming fire" (Heb. 12:29), and that fire could have consumed the people! How does Jesus' sacrifice protect us from being consumed when we approach God?

From the Commentary

A day which should have ended with the glorious worship of Jehovah God was instead climaxed with the funeral of two of Aaron's sons.

Everything that these two men did was wrong. To begin with, they were *the wrong people* to be handling the incense and presenting it to the Lord. This was the task of their father, the high priest (Ex. 30:7–10). They also used the *wrong instruments*, their own censers instead of the censer of the high priest, sanctified by the special anointing oil (40:9). They acted at *the wrong time*, for it was only on the annual Day of Atonement that the high priest was permitted to take incense into the Holy of Holies, and even then he had to submit to a special ritual (Lev. 16:1ff.).

They acted under the *wrong authority*. They didn't consult with Moses or their father, nor did they seek to follow the Word of God, which Moses had received. In burning the incense, they used the *wrong fire*, what Scripture calls "strange fire" (10:1; NIV says "unauthorized fire"). The high priest was commanded to burn the incense on coals taken from the brazen altar (16:12), but Nadab and Abihu supplied their own fire, and God rejected it. They acted from *the wrong motive* and didn't seek to glorify God alone (10:3).

Finally, they depended on *the wrong energy*, for verses 9–10 imply that they were under the influence of alcohol. This reminds us of Ephesians 5:18, "And be not drunk with wine ... but be filled with the Spirit."

—*Be Holy*, pages 48–49

10. What might have prompted Aaron's sons to act the way they did? Did they desire to sanctify and glorify the Lord or to promote themselves? Explain. How do their actions reflect the way some believers choose to act today? How are the results similar?

Looking Inward

Take a moment to reflect on all that you've explored thus far in this study of Leviticus 8—10. Review your notes and answers and think about how each of these things matters in your life today.

Tips for Small Groups: To get the most out of this section, form pairs or trios and have group members take turns answering these questions. Be honest and as open as you can in this discussion, but most of all, be encouraging and supportive of others. Be sensitive to those who are going through particularly difficult times and don't press for people to speak if they're uncomfortable doing so.

11. What are some ways your church acts as the holy nation God wants it to be? What are some things that hamper progress toward that goal? What role do you play in helping the local church to be a holy nation?

12. Are you easily drawn to religious fads and novelties? Why or why not? What measure do you use to determine if a church program is God honoring and biblical? What is your response if you find something in the church that appears to be nonbiblical?

13. Describe a time when pride got you in trouble. What was it about feeling "important" that led you to act the way you did? What was the right response in that situation?

Going Forward

14. Think of one or two things that you have learned that you'd like to work on in the coming week. Remember that this is all about quality, not quantity. It's better to work on one specific area of life and do it well than to work on many and do poorly (or to be so overwhelmed that you simply don't try).

Do you want to address pride in your life? Be specific. Go back through Leviticus 8—10 and put a star next to the phrase or verse that is most encouraging to you. Consider memorizing this verse.

Real-Life Application Ideas: Meet with church leaders to review the programs and ministry opportunities offered in your church. Talk together about how each one honors God and helps bring people closer to Him. If in the process you discover something that appears to be more of a fad or a novelty, discuss ways to make that program more God honoring or biblical. Keep in mind that God honoring might mean reaching outside the church walls and serving in ways that don't appear on the surface to be spiritual in nature. God works in many ways.

Seeking Help

15. Write a prayer below (or simply pray one in silence), inviting God to work on your mind and heart in those areas you've noted in the Going Forward section. Be honest about your desires and fears.

Notes for Small Groups:
- *Look for ways to put into practice the things you wrote in the Going Forward section. Talk with other group members about your ideas and commit to being accountable to one another.*
- *During the coming week, ask the Holy Spirit to continue to reveal truth to you from what you've read and studied.*
- *Before you start the next lesson, read Leviticus 11—12. For more in-depth lesson preparation, read chapter 4, "Cleanliness and Godliness," in* Be Holy.

Godliness
(LEVITICUS 11—12)

Before you begin …
- *Pray for the Holy Spirit to reveal truth and wisdom as you go through this lesson.*
- *Read Leviticus 11—12. This lesson references chapter 4 in Be Holy. It will be helpful for you to have your Bible and a copy of the commentary available as you work through this lesson.*

Getting Started

From the Commentary

"Cleanliness is next to godliness." John Wesley is generally credited with that saying, but it's likely the proverb was current before his time. In fact, the way Wesley quoted it in his sermon "On Dress" indicates that his listeners were already familiar with the maxim.

The Jews would readily identify with the saying; in the camp of Israel, the concepts of *cleanliness* and *godliness* were so intertwined that they were almost synonymous. The Jews feared lest they become ceremonially unclean because of something they had touched or eaten. From birth to burial, the Jews had to submit every aspect of their daily lives to the authority of God's law. Whether it was selecting their food, preparing their food, caring for a mother and new baby, diagnosing a disease, or disposing of waste, nothing was left to chance in the camp of Israel lest someone be defiled. In order to maintain ceremonial purity, each Jew had to obey God's law in several areas of life.

—*Be Holy*, page 55

1. Why do Leviticus and the other Old Testament books place such a heavy emphasis on cleanliness? How is cleanliness a good emblem or picture of holiness? What are the risks of overemphasizing the idea of cleanliness? What are the risks of underestimating its importance?

More to Consider: Whether a creature was "clean" or "unclean" had nothing to do with the quality of the beast; it all depended on what God said about the animal. When He gave these laws, no doubt the Lord had the health of His people in mind (Ex. 15:26; Deut. 7:15). But what was the main purpose of the dietary code? (See Lev. 11:44.) How did it fulfill that purpose?

2. Choose one verse or phrase from Leviticus 11—12 that stands out to you. This could be something you're intrigued by, something that makes you uncomfortable, something that puzzles you, something that resonates with you, or just something you want to examine further. Write that here.

Going Deeper

From the Commentary

> "For you were bought at a price; therefore glorify God in your body and in your spirit, which are God's" (1 Cor. 6:20 NKJV). "Therefore, whether you eat or drink, or whatever you do, do all to the glory of God" (10:31 NKJV).
>
> Three facts should be noted about the dietary laws: (1) God gave these laws only to the Jewish nation; (2)

obeying them guaranteed ceremonial purity but didn't automatically make the person holy in character; and (3) the laws were temporary and were ended on the cross of Christ (Col. 2:14).

—*Be Holy*, page 56

3. How does the spiritual principle of separation from defilement apply to the people of God today? What has God given the church today in lieu of a list of things that are clean and unclean? How do we know what pleases or grieves Him?

From the Commentary

Jesus made it clear to His disciples that all foods were clean (Mark 7:1ff.), and God taught this lesson again to Peter before He sent him to minister to the "unclean" Gentiles (Acts 10:9–16). Paul affirmed that special days and diets must not be considered either the *means* or the *measure* of a person's spirituality (Rom. 14:1—15:13).

—*Be Holy*, page 56

4. Read 1 Corinthians 8:8; Colossians 2:16–23; and 1 Timothy 4:1–5. What did Paul say in these verses about the role of food in relationship to God? How is this similar to what is taught in Leviticus? How is it different?

From Today's World

Today's church doesn't follow many of the old dietary rules from Leviticus, primarily because of how different our culture is from that of Moses' time, but also because of the change that Jesus brought with His message of grace. But there are a number of Old Testament laws and regulations that church leaders do abide by, and still more that leaders struggle to understand in today's culture. Dietary guidelines may be considered relatively minor in the grand scheme of things, but many of the other laws are controversial enough to divide a church.

5. How does a church determine which Old Testament laws are still valid today and which aren't? Why is this such a divisive issue in the church today? What "filters" should our churches use to determine whether something is worth fighting a theological battle over?

From the Commentary

> The Jews under the old covenant had to learn to despise the foods that God said were unclean and to enjoy the foods that God said were clean. It was a choice between pleasing themselves and being unclean or pleasing the Lord and being clean. There was no middle ground. If any food was questionable, it should have been automatically rejected, lest they disobey God and defile themselves.
>
> —*Be Holy*, page 58

6. How is the idea of choosing between pleasing yourself and pleasing God applicable in both Old Testament times and New Testament times? What does this decision point teach us about holiness? About selfishness? About where we're to find our direction in life?

From the Commentary

> The emphasis in Leviticus 11:24–43 is on avoiding the defilement caused by touching certain dead creatures, both clean and unclean. If a Jew happened upon the carcass of even a clean animal, he knew it was defiled

because the blood hadn't been properly drained out nor had the meat been protected from contamination. When Samson ate the honey from the carcass of the lion, he defiled himself and ceased to be a Nazirite (Judg. 14:1–9; see Num. 6:6, 9). No matter how sweet the honey was, it was unclean in God's sight; this made Samson unclean.

People who became defiled from touching a carcass were considered unclean until the end of the day. They had to wash themselves and their clothes and couldn't enter the camp until sunset. This kept them from spreading to others any contamination they might have picked up from touching the dead animal. If a dead creature fell into an earthen vessel, the vessel was smashed. Anything touched by the carcass was unclean and had to be either washed or destroyed.

—*Be Holy*, pages 58–59

7. What were the hygienic reasons behind these regulations? What was the spiritual reason? How is Paul's admonition of the Corinthians a contemporary application of this principle? (See 2 Cor. 6:14—7:1.)

From the Commentary

God said that the tree in the midst of the garden was off-limits to the man and woman, but Eve "saw that the tree was good for food" (Gen. 3:6) and took the fruit. God said that all the spoil of Jericho was under divine restriction and not to be touched by the Jewish soldiers (Josh. 6:16–19), but Achan revised that classification and took some of the spoil (7:16–26). It cost him his life. Samuel told King Saul to slay all the Amalekites and their flocks and herds, but the king kept Agag alive and kept "the best of the sheep and of the oxen" to give to the Lord (1 Sam. 15:15). Saul reclassified what God had said was abominable and thought this would make it acceptable, but his folly caused him to lose his kingdom.

—*Be Holy*, pages 59–60

8. In what ways is our society today one of moral relativism, where people feel they can shape their own moral codes? How does this go against what God taught in Leviticus? How does it go against what Jesus taught in Matthew 5:17–48?

More to Consider: In Leviticus 11, the words "unclean" and "detest" are used frequently. What does the context in which these words are used tell us about God? (See also Isa. 5:20.) What does it tell us about sin? How do people in all generations attempt to make sin acceptable by reclassifying it?

From the Commentary

If the Jewish people were to keep themselves clean and pleasing to the Lord, they had to exercise discernment; this meant knowing God's Word, respecting it, and obeying it. Fathers and mothers had to teach their children the law and warn them about the things that were unclean (Deut. 6:1–9). The priests had to teach the people and remind them of the commandments of the Lord. It was when the nation of Israel neglected the Word of God and refused to obey it that the people began to follow the abominable practices of the heathen nations around them, and this is what led to Israel's discipline and defeat.

The Jews had to remind themselves every hour of every day that they belonged to Jehovah, the true and living God, and that belonging to the nation of Israel was a high and holy privilege. "I am the LORD your God; consecrate yourselves and be holy, because I am holy" (Lev. 11:44 NIV). In New Testament language, "Walk worthy of the calling with which you were called" (Eph. 4:1 NKJV). Obeying God's will isn't a burden; it's a privilege! As Moses reminded his people, "For what great nation is there that has God so near to it, as the LORD our God is to us, for whatever reason we may call upon Him? And what great nation is there that has such statutes and righteous judgments as are in all this law which I set before you this day?" (Deut. 4:7–8 NKJV).

—*Be Holy*, page 61

9. Review Leviticus 11:44–47. What role does discernment play in these verses? What does it mean to exercise discernment? How do we need to practice that in the church today? Why is it so tempting to follow the ways of the world? How does following the ways of the world affect our pursuit of holiness?

From the Commentary

In giving birth to a baby, the mother experienced bleeding (Lev. 12:4–5, 7), as well as the secretion of other bodily fluids (see chap. 15), and this made her *ceremonially* unclean. The theme of Leviticus 12 is not personal holiness but *ritual* purification for the mother, without which she could not return to normal life in her home and in the camp.

Therefore, nothing in Leviticus 12 should be interpreted to teach that human sexuality is "dirty," that pregnancy is defiling, or that babies are impure. God created humans "male and female" (Gen. 1:27), and when God declared His creation to be "very good" (v. 31), that declaration included sex. He commanded our first parents to "be fruitful, and multiply" (v. 28); in spite of contemporary negative attitudes toward babies, Scripture presents children as blessings from God (Ps. 113:9; 127:3–5; 128:3; Prov. 17:6; Matt. 19:14). If for some reason a pregnancy was unwanted, the Jews would never consider aborting the baby.

—Be Holy, pages 63–64

10. What was the purpose of all these instructions for mothers in Leviticus 12? Why was ritual purification so important to the Israelites? To God? What are some ceremonies we perform today that carry a similar significance? How might a ceremonial act be a form of holiness?

Looking Inward

Take a moment to reflect on all that you've explored thus far in this study of Leviticus 11—12. Review your notes and answers and think about how each of these things matters in your life today.

Tips for Small Groups: To get the most out of this section, form pairs or trios and have group members take turns answering these questions. Be honest and as open as you can in this discussion, but most of all, be encouraging and supportive of others. Be sensitive to those who are going through particularly difficult times and don't press for people to speak if they're uncomfortable doing so.

11. What role does distinguishing between clean and unclean things play in your life? Is there a spiritual application in that? If so, what is it? How do you live that message out practically?

12. What do you think about the dietary rules practiced by the Israelites (and also to a great degree by many Jews today)? What is the lesson inherent in those rules? How can you apply that lesson to your life today?

13. What are some of the areas of life where you struggle to follow God rather than the ways of the world? What helps you choose well? What can get in the way?

Going Forward

14. Think of one or two things that you have learned that you'd like to work on in the coming week. Remember that this is all about quality, not quantity. It's better to work on one specific area of life and do it well than to work on many and do poorly (or to be so overwhelmed that you simply don't try).

Do you want to get rid of something unclean in your life? Be specific. Go back through Leviticus 11—12 and put a star next to the phrase or verse that is most encouraging to you. Consider memorizing this verse.

Real-Life Application Ideas: This week, see if you can abide by the dietary laws that the Jews were given in Leviticus. (This could drastically change your diet, so be prepared.) There are a number of good resources online to help you with this. Don't make this experience into a game or merely do it to see if you can. Instead, take each meal seriously and use the new perspective provided by making such a change to spend time with God, thanking Him for caring so much about His people that He would guide them in all areas of life.

Seeking Help

15. Write a prayer below (or simply pray one in silence), inviting God to work on your mind and heart in those areas you've noted in the Going Forward section. Be honest about your desires and fears.

Notes for Small Groups:

- *Look for ways to put into practice the things you wrote in the Going Forward section. Talk with other group members about your ideas and commit to being accountable to one another.*

- *During the coming week, ask the Holy Spirit to continue to reveal truth to you from what you've read and studied.*

- *Before you start the next lesson, read Leviticus 13—16. For more in-depth lesson preparation, read chapters 5 and 6, "The Great Physician" and "Israel's High and Holy Day," in* Be Holy.

The Physician
(LEVITICUS 13—16)

Before you begin ...
- *Pray for the Holy Spirit to reveal truth and wisdom as you go through this lesson.*
- *Read Leviticus 13—16. This lesson references chapters 5 and 6 in* Be Holy. *It will be helpful for you to have your Bible and a copy of the commentary available as you work through this lesson.*

Getting Started

From the Commentary

Leviticus 13—15 illustrates three topics that are vitally related to the life of holiness: sin (chap. 13), salvation (chap. 14), and sanctity (chap. 15).

Since infection made a person ceremonially unclean, God appointed the priests to act as His examiners to determine whether the victim was unclean and therefore had to be separated from the rest of the camp. The person being examined could be isolated for as long as two weeks to give the disease a chance to change for better or for worse. The symptoms might involve swelling and a rash (13:1–8); swelling, whiteness, and raw flesh (vv. 9–17); boils (vv. 18–23); burns (vv. 24–28); and various skin eruptions (vv. 29–44). Not everything that looked like leprosy actually was leprosy, and it would be cruel to isolate somebody who wasn't actually infected.

—*Be Holy*, page 70

1. Why did the investigation of leprosy include not only persons (Lev. 13:1–46) but also clothing (vv. 47–49) and even houses (14:33–57)? What was the literal point of these instructions? What is the spiritual message here?

More to Consider: The Hebrew word translated "infectious skin disease" in Leviticus 14 includes various diseases and even mildew (13:47–59; 14:33–57). But there's more to these chapters than simply a description of symptoms and ceremonies. Read Psalm 147:3; Isaiah 1:5–6; Jeremiah 8:2; 30:12; and Mark 2:17. How does each of these passages use the image of disease to reference the concept of sin?

2. Choose one verse or phrase from Leviticus 13—16 that stands out to you. This could be something you're intrigued by, something that makes you uncomfortable, something that puzzles you, something that resonates with you, or just something you want to examine further. Write that here.

Going Deeper

From the Commentary

"The heart is deceitful above all things, and desperately wicked: who can know it?" (Jer. 17:9). The word translated "wicked" in this verse means "sick"; the NIV translates it "beyond cure." Sin is not a surface problem that can be solved with simple remedies, like trying to cure cancer with hand lotion. Sin comes from within, from fallen human nature; unless the heart is changed, there can be no solving of the sin problem. "For I know that in me (that is, in my flesh) nothing good dwells" (Rom. 7:18 NKJV). Those who talk about the "innate goodness of man" know neither the Bible nor their own hearts.

In eighteenth-century England, if you were convicted for stealing, the judge could order the authorities to chop off your right hand. If you were convicted a second time, they could cut off the left hand. I recall reading about a pickpocket who lost both hands but managed to succeed in his career because he perfected picking pockets *with his teeth!* Even if the authorities had pulled all his teeth, it wouldn't have solved the problem, because sin is deeper than the skin. Jesus said, "For out of the heart proceed evil thoughts, murders, adulteries, fornications, thefts, false witness, blasphemies: These are the things which defile a man" (Matt. 15:19–20).

In Jeremiah's day, the false prophets were like physicians who lied to their patients and refused to give them bad news. "They have healed also the hurt of the daughter of my people slightly, saying, Peace, peace; when there is no peace" (Jer. 6:14). The medical profession today would discipline a doctor who did that, but the practice is perfectly acceptable for humanistic counselors, liberal preachers and professors, politicians, and newspaper columnists. People still believe the "progress myth" that people are good and are making themselves and the world better and better day by day.

—*Be Holy*, pages 70–71

3. What does the phrase "sin is deeper than skin" mean? Where does sin root itself? Why does Leviticus focus so much on identifying sin and on the proper way to deal with it? In what ways does the modern church focus on sin?

From the Commentary

> The word *unclean* is used fifty-four times in Leviticus
> 13—15. It describes the ceremonial defilement that
> makes the victim unfit for social life or for participation
> in worship at the house of God. The prophet Isaiah con-
> fessed that he was "a man of unclean lips" (Isa. 6:5), and
> then he spoke for all of us when he wrote, "But we are all
> as an unclean thing, and all our righteousnesses are as
> filthy rags" (64:6). Whatever sin touches, it defiles; only
> the blood of Jesus Christ can wash away that defilement
> (1 Cor. 6:9–11; 1 John 1:7; Rev. 1:5).
>
> —*Be Holy*, page 72

4. Read Psalm 51. What does David's confession teach us about being
defiled by sin? How did it affect him? How does sin defile us?

From the Commentary

> What solemn words in Leviticus 13:46: "He is unclean:
> he shall dwell alone; without the camp shall his habita-
> tion be." He had to tear his clothes, put a covering on

his upper lip, cry "Unclean, unclean!" whenever anybody approached him, and remain outside the camp until either he died or was healed. "Free among the dead" is the way Heman described it in Psalm 88:5. God struck King Azariah (Uzziah) with leprosy, and he had to dwell in a "separate house," literally "a free house," which was isolated from everybody else (2 Kings 15:5 NIV). He was free—among the dead!

—Be Holy, page 73

5. How are sinners like the lepers who had to live outside of populated areas in Bible times? Why is isolation such a significant consequence of sin? Why is isolation so dangerous to our relationship with God? How do we find our way out of the isolation that sin brings?

From the Commentary

The steps in the leper's cleansing and restoration picture to us what Jesus Christ has done for sinners.

When He ministered here on earth, Jesus was called "a friend of publicans and sinners" (Luke 7:34); He compared Himself to a doctor helping his needy patients (Matt.

9:10–13). As God's Great Physician, Jesus makes "house calls" and comes to sinners right where they are. In the case of the Jewish leper, the priest went out to investigate and determine if indeed the victim was healed, but Jesus comes to us that He might heal us of the sickness of sin.

The unusual ritual of offering two birds (Lev. 14:4–7) pictures to us what Christ did to save a lost world. Birds don't belong in clay jars; they belong in the heavens. Jesus came down from heaven and became a man (John 3:13, 31; 6:38, 42). As it were, He put Himself into a clay jar so that He might die for our sins. The running water over which the bird was killed reminds us of the Holy Spirit of God (John 7:37–39), for Jesus offered Himself to God "through the eternal Spirit" (Heb. 9:14). When the blood-stained living bird was turned loose, it pictured our Lord's resurrection, for the resurrection of Christ is as much a part of the gospel message as is His death (1 Cor. 15:1–4). Only a living Savior can save dead sinners.

The blood of the bird that was sacrificed was in the jar and on the living bird, but it also had to be applied to the healed leper. Using the hyssop (Ex. 12:22; Ps. 51:7), the priest sprinkled the blood on the leper seven times and then pronounced the leper clean. "Without shedding of blood is no remission" (Heb. 9:22). How did the victim know he was clean? The priest told him so! How do believers today know that God has saved us? He tells us so in His Word! No matter how the leper felt or what he looked like, God said he was clean, and that settled it.

On the day of his cleansing, the leper had to wash himself and his garments and shave off all his hair. He was then permitted to enter the camp, but he wasn't allowed to enter his tent. He had to stay outside for another week.

Why wash when the priest had already pronounced him clean? Because he had to apply *personally* what God said was true *positionally*. The man was ceremonially clean and had the *right* to live in the camp, but he needed to be made personally and practically clean so he would be *fit* to live in the camp. "Wash yourselves, make yourselves clean" (Isa. 1:16 NKJV). "Let us cleanse ourselves from all filthiness of the flesh and spirit, perfecting holiness in the fear of God" (2 Cor. 7:1). Perhaps Paul had Leviticus 14 in mind when he compared the new life in Christ to a change of clothes (Col. 3:1–14).

A week later, the man must cleanse himself again. The man had to wash, shave his body again, and put on clean clothes. The dual shaving left his skin like that of a baby, perhaps symbolizing a new birth. The shaving and washing didn't kill the germs of leprosy—God had done that—but they symbolized the newness of life that had come to the former leper.

The person offered the required sacrifices (Lev. 14:10–32). It's now the eighth day since the priest first visited the leper, and eight is the number of the new beginning. The cleansed leper must bring to the door of the tabernacle a male lamb for a trespass (guilt) offering, a male lamb for a burnt offering, a ewe lamb for a sin offering, as well as fine flour and oil for a meal offering.

—*Be Holy*, pages 74–76

6. Why was the priest needed to pronounce the man clean (Lev. 14:7)? In what ways do these cleansing sacrifices picture the person and work of Jesus Christ? Why is it important to connect the laws in Leviticus with the life of Christ? What does this tell us about God's plan for His people?

From the Commentary

The key word in Leviticus 15 is *issue*, used twenty-four times. It simply means a flow of liquid, whether water in nature or a fluid discharged from the human body. The human discharge may be natural (vv. 16–18, 25–30) or unnatural (vv. 1–15, 19–24), but it's still considered unclean and must be dealt with according to the law of God. Personal hygiene and God's concern for women are certainly involved in these regulations, but the main thrust seems to be that of enforcing personal sanctity.

Not everybody is a leper, but all of us have occasional "discharges" that defile us and could defile others.

—*Be Holy,* page 77

7. Review Leviticus 15. In what ways were these regulations for personal sanctity more than pious suggestions from the religious leaders? What was the result of disobeying these regulations (vv. 24, 31–33)? Why were the punishments so serious? What does that tell us about the worldly culture of the time?

From the Commentary

The most important day of the year for the Old Testament Jew was the Day of Atonement—Yom Kippur—when God graciously atoned for all the sins of all the people and gave the nation a new beginning. Because today they have neither a temple nor a priest (Hos. 3:4), Israel can't celebrate Yom Kippur in the appointed way, but those who have received Jesus Christ can see in this ancient ritual a picture of what Jesus did for us on the cross.

God made it clear that the priests should not be afraid to serve, but that only the high priest was to enter the

Holy of Holies, and that only once a year on the Day of Atonement. It wasn't a matter of human choice; it was a matter of divine appointment. Any priest who disobeyed would die.

—*Be Holy*, page 83

8. Review Leviticus 16:1–2, 29–30. How might the deaths of Nadab and Abihu (Lev. 10) have affected the work of Aaron and the priests? Why did God have a rule about who could enter the Holy of Holies on the Day of Atonement? What was the spiritual purpose of this very specific law? (See Heb. 9:7–15.)

More to Consider: On the first day of the seventh month, the trumpets were blown to announce the beginning of a new year (Rosh Hashanah; Lev. 23:23–25). The tenth day was the Day of Atonement (vv. 26–32), and then came the Feast of Tabernacles (or Booths), which started on the fifteenth day of the month and lasted a week (vv. 33–44). Why was the timing of these days so important to the Israelites? What spiritual lesson were they being taught by each of the days? By the way the days were arranged?

From the Commentary

> The Hebrew word *kapar*, translated "atonement," is used fifteen times in Leviticus 16, and it basically means "to ransom, to remove by paying a price." The priest placed his hands on the head of the sacrifice, symbolizing the transferring of the nation's sins to the innocent victim who died in their place. Atonement means that a price is paid and blood is shed, because life must be given for life (17:11). John Stott says it magnificently: "We strongly reject, therefore, every explanation of the death of Christ which does not have at its center the principle of 'satisfaction through substitution,' indeed divine self-satisfaction through divine self-substitution."
>
> The word *blood* is used nine times in Leviticus 16 and thirteen times in chapter 17. If the Day of Atonement teaches us anything about salvation, it's that there can be no salvation from sin apart from the shedding of blood. Those who reject this view and claim that they want "only the loving religion of Jesus" had better listen to what Jesus Himself said: "For this is My blood of the new covenant, which is shed for many for the remission of sins" (Matt. 26:28 NKJV). "Just as the Son of Man did not come to be served, but to serve, and to give His life a ransom for many" (Matt. 20:28 NKJV).
>
> —*Be Holy*, pages 84–85

9. Take note of the words "blood" and "atonement" in Leviticus 16. What does this repetition alone tell you about the message here? How is this message similar to what we discover in the New Testament about Jesus?

From the Commentary

Many see in the annual Day of Atonement a picture of Israel's future cleansing when their Messiah appears to deliver them, cleanse them, and establish them in their kingdom.

The seventh month begins with the blowing of the trumpets, and there is a future "trumpet call" for Israel to gather the people together. "And it shall come to pass in that day that the Lord will thresh, from the channel of the River to the Brook of Egypt; and you will be gathered one by one, O you children of Israel. So it shall be in that day: The great trumpet will be blown; they will come, who are about to perish in the land of Assyria, and they who are outcasts in the land of Egypt, and shall worship the Lord in the holy mount at Jerusalem" (Isa. 27:12–13 NKJV). Jesus also referred to this future gathering of the Jews (Matt. 24:29–31).

—*Be Holy*, page 89

10. Read Zechariah 12:10—13:1. How might this be a reference to the Messiah? In what ways will the people mourn when they see their Messiah? Why will they mourn rather than celebrate?

Looking Inward

Take a moment to reflect on all that you've explored thus far in this study of Leviticus 13—16. Review your notes and answers and think about how each of these things matters in your life today.

Tips for Small Groups: To get the most out of this section, form pairs or trios and have group members take turns answering these questions. Be honest and as open as you can in this discussion, but most of all, be encouraging and supportive of others. Be sensitive to those who are going through particularly difficult times and don't press for people to speak if they're uncomfortable doing so.

11. Recall the phrase "sin is deeper than skin." How do you see this evident in your life? What steps do you take to make sure you're dealing with the root of sin, not just the evidence of sin?

12. Have you ever felt defiled by your sin? Explain. How does God's grace speak to that feeling? How does it affect you to think that shed blood has atoned for your sin?

13. In Moses' day, access to God was limited to the priests. How would you feel today if your access to God were only available secondhand? What are some ways you encounter God "face-to-face" today?

Going Forward

14. Think of one or two things that you have learned that you'd like to work on in the coming week. Remember that this is all about quality, not quantity. It's better to work on one specific area of life and do it well than to work on many and do poorly (or to be so overwhelmed that you simply don't try).

Do you want to respond to the fact that your sins have been atoned for and you are clean before God? Be specific. Go back through Leviticus 13—16 and put a star next to the phrase or verse that is most encouraging to you. Consider memorizing this verse.

Real-Life Application Ideas: This week, take time to thank God that Jesus' life, death, and resurrection made God accessible to everyone who seeks Him out. Use every possible opportunity to talk to God this week—from the most mundane activities (brushing your teeth, making your bed, cleaning up the kitchen) to the most notable events (celebrating a birth, sharing your faith with a friend, participating in corporate worship). Be aware as you engage in prayerful dialogue with the God of the universe that it wasn't always this way. Then end the week with a commitment to continue a more open and frequent conversation with God. Jesus made this amazing thing possible—why not use this access at all times?

Seeking Help

15. Write a prayer below (or simply pray one in silence), inviting God to work on your mind and heart in those areas you've noted in the Going Forward section. Be honest about your desires and fears.

Notes for Small Groups:

- *Look for ways to put into practice the things you wrote in the Going Forward section. Talk with other group members about your ideas and commit to being accountable to one another.*
- *During the coming week, ask the Holy Spirit to continue to reveal truth to you from what you've read and studied.*
- *Before you start the next lesson, read Leviticus 17—20. For more in-depth lesson preparation, read chapter 7, "Holiness Is a Practical Thing," in* Be Holy.

Holiness
(LEVITICUS 17—20)

Before you begin ...
- *Pray for the Holy Spirit to reveal truth and wisdom as you go through this lesson.*
- *Read Leviticus 17—20. This lesson references chapter 7 in* Be Holy. *It will be helpful for you to have your Bible and a copy of the commentary available as you work through this lesson.*

Getting Started

From the Commentary

Leviticus 17—20 constituted a legal code for the people of Israel, touching on many areas of their personal and public life. The emphasis isn't simply on justice or civic righteousness, as important as they are, but on *holiness.* After all, Israel was *God's* people and the law was *God's* law. The Lord said to them, "Consecrate yourselves therefore, and be holy, for I am the LORD your God. And you

shall keep My statutes, and perform them: I am the LORD
who sanctifies you" (20:7–8 NKJV).

—*Be Holy*, pages 93–94

1. What was the motivation for Israel's obedience? (See Ex. 19:3–6.) Why
was it important that this motivation be more than fear of punishment?
How does the following statement apply to the Israelites' circumstances:
Obeying the law and having holy character aren't necessarily the same
thing. How does it apply to believers today?

*More to Consider: Twenty-four times in these four chapters we find
the declaration "I am the LORD." How does this declaration show
God's right to give laws? How is it a motivation for obedience? How
is holiness related to this declaration of who God is?*

2. Choose one verse or phrase from Leviticus 17—20 that stands out to
you. This could be something you're intrigued by, something that makes
you uncomfortable, something that puzzles you, something that resonates
with you, or just something you want to examine further. Write that here.

Going Deeper

From the Commentary

> Leviticus 17—20 deals with four special areas of life
> that must be respected and kept holy: the sanctity of
> blood, or life (chap. 17); the sanctity of sex (chap. 18);
> the sanctity of the law (chap. 19); and the sanctity of
> judgment (chap. 20).
>
> —*Be Holy*, page 94

3. What makes each of the four areas mentioned in the previous
commentary excerpt notable in the pursuit of holiness? Why these four
areas and not others? How does the message in Leviticus 17—20 apply to
believers today?

From the Commentary

> According to Leon Morris, the word *blood* is used 460
> times in the Bible, 362 of them in the Old Testament. In
> Leviticus 17, you find the word "blood" 13 times; you also
> find in this chapter the key text in biblical theology on the
> significance of the blood in salvation: "For the life of the

flesh is in the blood, and I have given it to you upon the altar to make atonement for your souls; for it is the blood that makes atonement for the soul" (v. 11 NKJV).

Long before medical science discovered the significance of the circulation of the blood in the human body and its importance for life, Scripture told us that the blood was the life. When a sacrifice was offered and its blood was shed, it meant the giving of a life for the life of another. The innocent victim died in the place of the guilty sinner.

—*Be Holy*, pages 94–95

4. Why is blood such an important symbol in the Old Testament story? Why is it important in the New Testament story? What role does it play in sacrifice? Atonement? Can you have an orthodox Christian theology without this important theme? Why or why not?

From Today's World

One of the more contentious themes in the Bible (in Leviticus, certainly, but also elsewhere) is the sanctity of sex. It's not a contentious theme because Christians think of it as controversial, but because many simply find it difficult to discuss. To talk about sex in the context of faith is awkward at best. Yet it continues to be a hot topic because the world has a very different idea about what sex ought to be or is allowed to be. The absence of intentional conversation on this subject in the church makes it difficult for Christians to separate what the world teaches from what God teaches.

5. Why is the church so uncomfortable with exploring the subject of sex and sexuality? What does the Bible teach us about the importance of this topic? What are some ways the church can address the issue without embarrassment? Why is it critical to the health of the church?

From the Commentary

> We live in a sex-saturated society. It smiles at monogamous marriages, encourages abortion as a means of birth control, promotes and endorses kinky sex as a means of entertainment, claims that moral absolutes don't exist, and really believes that people can violate moral standards and escape the consequences. Fulton J. Sheen was right when he said, "The Victorians pretended [sex] did not exist; the moderns pretend that nothing else exists."
>
> There are several reasons why the Lord gives clear instructions concerning personal sexual hygiene, sexual morality, and marriage. For one thing, we're created in the image of God, and the Creator knows what's best for His creation.

God certainly wants married couples to enjoy the beautiful gift of sex, but He also wants them to avoid the terrible consequences that come when His laws are violated.

—*Be Holy*, page 97

6. Review Leviticus 18:1–5, which stresses the importance of obedience. Now read Nehemiah 9:29; Luke 10:28; Romans 10:5; and Galatians 3:12. In these verses, why did the authors repeat Moses' words? What were they trying to convey about God's law? Can obedience save us? If not, then why do these verses and similar passages in Scripture emphasize it? What does our obedience reveal about our hearts?

From the Commentary

The picture in Leviticus 18:24–30 isn't a pretty one. Sexual perversions are like disease germs; they make a society and a nation sick. Then the land itself becomes sick and must vomit out its filthy people the way a human body vomits out poison. How tragic that people made in God's image should end up as vomit! Please note that these were Gentile nations that were judged—peoples with whom God had not made any covenants, but He still held them accountable for their filthy deeds against nature (Rom. 1:18ff.).

—*Be Holy*, page 100

7. What were some of the consequences of sexual sin for the Israelites? What are the consequences today? How does sexual sin make a society sick? What is the cure?

From the Commentary

In Leviticus 19, the Ten Commandments are applied to various areas of life; in Leviticus 20, the penalties are stated that must be imposed on those who disobey His commandments. God expected His people to take His law seriously and to apply the penalties obediently and without favoritism.

The regulations given in Leviticus 19 aren't arranged in any discernible order, but the one thing that ties them together is their relationship to the Ten Commandments (Ex. 20:1–17), which is the basis for all Jewish law and should be the basis for all moral law.

—*Be Holy*, page 100

8. Go through the regulations in Leviticus 19 and connect each of them to one of the Ten Commandments (Ex. 20:1–17). Why is this connection significant? Which of these regulations are applicable to us today? How do we know which are and which aren't?

More to Consider: Leviticus 19:3, 30 reminded the people of the fourth commandment (Ex. 20:8–11) and of the fact that the Sabbath was a special "sign" between God and Israel. What was it a sign of (Ex. 31:13–17)? Why was violating the Sabbath a capital offense? How important is it today that we take weekly time away from busyness to be restful and worship our Creator? Why?

From the Commentary

God's concern for the *poor and needy* is seen in the "harvest laws" (Lev. 19:9–10; see 23:22; Deut. 23:24–25; 24:19–22; Ruth 2). It is also seen in the regulation about wages (Lev. 19:13). Since workers were paid daily, any delay would cause hardship (Deut. 24:14–15; James

5:4), and employers must never take advantage of their employees.

The nation must be careful to have *just weights and measures*, lest unscrupulous merchants rob innocent people.

—*Be Holy*, page 102

9. In what ways do the rich and poor stand equal before God and the law (Lev. 19:15)? What does this tell us about justice? What are "just weights and measures" (Lev. 19:35–36)? How are these laws important to justice in the courts and the economy of today?

From the Commentary

Leviticus 20 states the penalties imposed on those who broke God's law. The same Lord who declared the precepts also declared the penalties.

Fifteen offenses in Israel were capital crimes: striking or cursing a parent (Ex. 21:15, 17); breaking the Sabbath (31:14); blaspheming God (Lev. 24:10–16); engaging in occult practices (Ex. 22:18); prophesying falsely (Deut. 13:1–5); adultery (Lev. 20:10); rape (Deut. 22:25);

unchastity before marriage (vv. 13ff.); incest (Lev. 20:11–12); homosexuality (v. 13); bestiality (vv. 15–16); kidnapping (Ex. 21:16); idolatry (Lev. 20:1–5); false witness in a case involving a capital crime (Deut. 19:16–21); killing a human intentionally (Ex. 21:12).

—Be Holy, pages 103–4

10. How is the Old Testament view of the offenses listed in the previous commentary excerpt different from the modern view? What was the purpose of God's law in relation to these offenses? Why did He impose such specific and drastic penalties? In a culture where the lack of technology and finances made it impossible to hold people in prisons for more than a few weeks, would monetary fines have been appropriate for serious crimes? Why or why not?

Looking Inward

Take a moment to reflect on all that you've explored thus far in this study of Leviticus 17—20. Review your notes and answers and think about how each of these things matters in your life today.

Tips for Small Groups: To get the most out of this section, form pairs or trios and have group members take turns answering these questions. Be honest and as open as you can in this discussion, but most of all, be encouraging and supportive of others. Be sensitive to those who are going through particularly difficult times and don't press for people to speak if they're uncomfortable doing so.

11. Leviticus has a repeating theme of obedience. How do you feel about this theme? What is it about obedience that makes you grow closer to God? What are the challenges of obeying God? How does your relationship with God determine your reaction to the very word *obedience*?

12. Do you think the church is doing a good enough job addressing the sanctity of sex? Explain. What has the church taught you about sex? What should the church teach?

13. Think about some of the sins you've committed. What were the physical consequences of those sins? The emotional or psychological consequences? What impact did those sins have on your spiritual life?

Going Forward

14. Think of one or two things that you have learned that you'd like to work on in the coming week. Remember that this is all about quality, not quantity. It's better to work on one specific area of life and do it well than to work on many and do poorly (or to be so overwhelmed that you simply don't try).

Do you want to take justice more seriously as something God values? Be specific. Go back through Leviticus 17—20 and put a star next to the phrase or verse that is most encouraging to you. Consider memorizing this verse.

Real-Life Application Ideas: This week, focus on the word sanctity. *Consider such topics as the sanctity of sex, of judgment, and of life, and think about what they mean to you. Then compare your belief about these topics with your actions. Are there some areas of life where you're falling short? What would it take to shore up that area of life? Consider talking with a trusted counselor or pastor about any area where you're really struggling, then dedicate yourself to working on that area as you seek to grow your relationship with God.*

Seeking Help

15. Write a prayer below (or simply pray one in silence), inviting God to work on your mind and heart in those areas you've noted in the Going Forward section. Be honest about your desires and fears.

Notes for Small Groups:

- *Look for ways to put into practice the things you wrote in the Going Forward section. Talk with other group members about your ideas and commit to being accountable to one another.*

- *During the coming week, ask the Holy Spirit to continue to reveal truth to you from what you've read and studied.*

- *Before you start the next lesson, read Leviticus 21—23. For more in-depth lesson preparation, read chapters 8 and 9, "The Cost of Spiritual Leadership" and "The Calendar That Tells the Future," in* Be Holy.

Leadership
(LEVITICUS 21—23)

Before you begin …
- *Pray for the Holy Spirit to reveal truth and wisdom as you go through this lesson.*
- *Read Leviticus 21—23. This lesson references chapters 8 and 9 in* Be Holy. *It will be helpful for you to have your Bible and a copy of the commentary available as you work through this lesson.*

Getting Started

From the Commentary

The spiritual leaders in the nation of Israel were the priests. "He shall not defile himself, being a chief man among his people" (Lev. 21:4 NKJV). They were in charge of the sanctuary of God; they taught the people the Word of God; they offered the sacrifices on God's altar; when called upon, they determined the will of God for the people. Apart from the ministry of the priests, Israel had no way to approach God.

The priests had to meet the qualifications God gave for the priesthood, and they had to serve Him according to His directions. In their personal conduct, physical characteristics, and professional concerns, they had to meet God's approval. There's a price to pay if you want to be a spiritual leader.

—*Be Holy*, page 109

1. What are some of the responsibilities that come with the privilege of leadership according to Leviticus? How is this similar to the responsibilities our leaders have today? Where did the priesthood in Israel go wrong? (See Hos. 4:8–9.) What was the punishment for leading people astray? Where do leaders today go wrong?

More to Consider: There were qualifications and requirements not only for the priests but also for every member of the priests' families. What was the most important requirement? (Consider the numerous instances of "unclean," "defile," and "profane" in Leviticus 21.) Why does the Lord say, "I am the Lord who makes you holy," or words to that effect, at the end of each section in Leviticus 21—22? (See 21:8, 15, 23; 22:9, 16, 32.)

2. Choose one verse or phrase from Leviticus 21—23 that stands out to you. This could be something you're intrigued by, something that makes you uncomfortable, something that puzzles you, something that resonates with you, or just something you want to examine further. Write that here.

Going Deeper

From the Commentary

> Since the high priest was especially anointed and clothed with holy garments (Lev. 8:7–12; 16:4), he had a greater obligation to serve the Lord faithfully and honor His name. The ordinary priests were permitted to be defiled by the dead bodies of their immediate family, but the high priest wasn't allowed to do even that. Nor was he

allowed to manifest grief in the usual ways or to leave the tabernacle precincts for a burial (see 10:6–7). Aaron and his sons had their tents on the east side of the tabernacle (Num. 3:38), and they were expected to stay on duty and not become involved in other activities in the camp (see 2 Tim. 2:4).

Since the firstborn son of the high priest became the next high priest, it was important that no alien issue invade the family; hence, the high priest could marry only a virgin (Lev. 21:13–14). In most cases, the priests chose their wives from the tribe of Levi (Luke 1:5), and this would be especially so with the high priest. To marry an unfit woman would defile his offspring, and this would defile the priesthood which the Lord God had sanctified (Lev. 21:8, 15).

—*Be Holy*, page 112

3. In what ways were these regulations specific to a culture and time? What are some modern principles that support these special regulations? How are these principles used today?

From the Commentary

Everyone born into Adam's race is a sinner, suffering from the tragic consequences of Adam's fall, but our physical and moral defects aren't an obstacle to either salvation or service. When God invites the lost to be saved, He calls to "the poor, the crippled, the blind and the lame" (Luke 14:21 NIV), the very people Jesus ministered to when He was here on earth (Matt. 4:23–25). And all believers can surrender to the Lord and be "living sacrifices" for His glory, no matter what handicaps they may have.

Fanny Crosby, the great hymn writer, was blind; so was George Matheson, author, hymn writer, and preacher. Amy Carmichael directed the work of her mission in India from her sickbed. The Scottish Presbyterian preacher Robert Murray McCheyne was often prostrated by his weak heart. And Charles Spurgeon had to leave London in the winter to restore his health in the south of France. Physical handicaps need not be a barrier to Christian service if we depend wholly on the grace of God (2 Cor. 12).

—*Be Holy*, page 113

4. Why did God require that every priest be free from defects and blemishes? How realistic an expectation was this? Explain. How is this similar to the expectations we put on today's leaders? How realistic are our expectations? How did Jesus' sacrifice change the expectations of leaders?

From the Commentary

> For a priest to serve the Lord acceptably, it wasn't enough
> that he qualify as a son of Aaron without any physical
> defects. He also had to carry on his ministry in such a
> way that the Lord was pleased with him. The worshippers
> might look at the outward ritual, but God would look at
> his inner heart.
>
> —*Be Holy*, page 115

5. Review Leviticus 22. In what ways does verse 2 set the theme for
this chapter? How does this quote from George MacDonald apply here:
"Nothing is so deadening to the divine as an habitual dealing with the
outsides of holy things"?

From the Commentary

> Suppose a priest became defiled but did nothing about
> it? How would anybody know that he was unclean? He
> could minister at the altar, handle the sacrifices, even eat
> his lawful share of the sacred offerings, and apparently

get away with it. But God would know it, and the priest would be in danger of death (Lev. 22:9).

This kind of behavior would indicate that the priest was putting himself ahead of God and was more concerned about his reputation than his character. The name for this sin is hypocrisy. It worried him that the people would know he was unclean, but it didn't worry him that he was defiling the sacred ministry for which God had set him apart. Like the Pharisees in our Lord's day, this priest appeared to be clean but was actually "toxic" (Matt. 23:25–28).

—*Be Holy*, page 116

6. Why is it important that all who serve the Lord and the Lord's people be open and honest before God? What does it look like to treat the things of God with holy respect? How does what Paul said in Acts 24:16 apply here? What protections against hypocrisy in ministry can we find in 2 Corinthians 1:12; 4:2; and 5:11?

From the Commentary

> The special requirement about the age of the offering (Lev. 22:26–28; see Ex. 22:30) shows the tender heart of the Creator toward His creation (Jonah 4:11; Deut. 22:6–7). A calf or lamb younger than a week old who was transported any distance to the sanctuary might die in the process. It seems to me that it would be cruel to kill the mother and her young on the same day, for whatever purposes.
>
> —*Be Holy*, page 118

7. What does God's care for the animals in this context reveal about His character? About how we ought to treat that with which God entrusts us (animals, the earth, etc.)?

From the Commentary

> The weekly Sabbath wasn't one of the annual feasts (Ex. 20:8–11), but it was an important day for the Jewish people, and they were expected to honor it. To dishonor it meant death (Num. 15:32–36).
>
> —*Be Holy*, page 124

8. Review Leviticus 23:1–3. Why did God give the Sabbath to Israel? (*Sabbath* comes from a Hebrew word that means "to rest, to cease from labor.") What does Genesis 2:1–3 tell us about the purpose of the Sabbath? What does Exodus 31:12–17 reveal? How did the New Testament story change the meaning of the Sabbath? (See Rom. 14:1–9; Col. 2:16–17.) How is the principle established in Leviticus and Exodus still valid today?

From the Commentary

Passover is Israel's feast of deliverance; the key passage is Exodus 12. The innocent lamb died for the firstborn; because the blood of the lamb was applied to the door by faith, the firstborn sons were safe. This was "the Lord's passover" and the only means of deliverance that He provided that awesome night when the death angel visited Egypt. To reject the blood of the lamb was to accept judgment and death.

The firstborn Jews in Egypt weren't saved from death by admiring the lamb, caring for the lamb, or loving the lamb. The lamb had to be slain, and the blood applied to the doorposts of each Jewish house. We aren't saved by Christ the Example or Christ the Teacher. We're saved by Christ the Substitute, who gave His life in our stead on the cross at the same hour the Passover lambs were being slain at the Jewish temple in Jerusalem.

—Be Holy, pages 125–26

9. Review Leviticus 23:4–5. In what ways did the Passover lamb typify Jesus Christ? (See John 1:29; 1 Cor. 5:7; 1 Peter 1:19–20.) The Passover lamb had to be perfect. How is this a very specific reference to Jesus? (See 2 Cor. 5:21; 1 Peter 2:22; 1 John 3:5.)

More to Consider: For seven days following Passover, the Jews ate only unleavened bread with their meals, and they carefully cleansed all the yeast out of their homes (Ex. 12:15–20). In many places in Scripture, leaven depicts sin. Thus the putting away of leaven illustrates the cleansing of one's life after he or she has been saved through faith in the blood (2 Cor. 6:14—7:1). What does it mean for us today to get rid of leaven? (See 1 Cor. 5:7.) What does it look like to put away the leaven of malice and wickedness (1 Cor. 5:8; Eph. 4:31–32), the leaven of hypocrisy (Luke 12:1), and the leaven of false doctrine (Gal. 5:7–9)?

From the Commentary

This special day was also called "the Feast of Weeks," because it was celebrated seven weeks after firstfruits. The word "Pentecost" means "fiftieth," and since the feast was held seven weeks after firstfruits, it too was on the first day of the week, the Lord's Day. Each Lord's Day commemorates the resurrection of Christ, the coming of the Spirit, and the birth of the church.

Instead of the priest waving *sheaves* before the Lord, he waved two *loaves* of bread baked with leaven. In order to have loaves, the grain had to be ground into flour and the flour baked into loaves. The fulfillment of this image is recorded in Acts 2 when fifty days after Christ's resurrection, the Holy Spirit came and united the believers into the church, symbolized here by the two loaves (Jews and Gentiles). There's leaven in the two loaves because there's sin in the church (Lev. 2:11). The church will not be "holy and without blemish" (Eph. 5:27) until it sees the Lord in glory.

The feast lasted only one day, a day on which the people were not to work but were to rejoice before the Lord and bring Him an offering commensurate with the harvest He had given them (Deut. 16:9–12). This event would have marked the end of the wheat harvest, and the Jews were commanded to remember the poor as they harvested the grain God had generously given them (Lev. 23:22; see Deut. 24:19–22).

—*Be Holy*, pages 128–29

10. How did the command in Leviticus 23:22 benefit Ruth? (See Ruth 2; 4.) What does this command teach us about God's love for the poor? How is Jesus' teaching on caring for the poor similar to what's expressed here? How is it different? (See for instance Matt. 25:31–46.)

Looking Inward

Take a moment to reflect on all that you've explored thus far in this study of Leviticus 21—23. Review your notes and answers and think about how each of these things matters in your life today.

Tips for Small Groups: To get the most out of this section, form pairs or trios and have group members take turns answering these questions. Be honest and as open as you can in this discussion, but most of all, be encouraging and supportive of others. Be sensitive to those who are going through particularly difficult times and don't press for people to speak if they're uncomfortable doing so.

11. Have you ever played the role of leader in your church? If so, describe that time. What did you think of carrying that responsibility? In what ways do leaders have to live up to a higher standard than others? What does that look like in practical terms?

12. To be holy means to be set apart. What are some ways you see yourself set apart because of your relationship with God? How does that affect your relationship with others? Should it? Explain.

13. Leviticus includes lots of rules and information about festivals and special days. What are some of the special days you celebrate because of your faith? How can those days help you grow closer to Christ? What are the dangers of putting too much emphasis on tradition or habit?

Going Forward

14. Think of one or two things that you have learned that you'd like to work on in the coming week. Remember that this is all about quality, not quantity. It's better to work on one specific area of life and do it well than to work on many and do poorly (or to be so overwhelmed that you simply don't try).

Do you want to do something for the poor? Be specific. Go back through Leviticus 21—23 and put a star next to the phrase or verse that is most encouraging to you. Consider memorizing this verse.

Real-Life Application Ideas: The many holy days and festivals the Israelites celebrated were all about their relationship with God. This week, work with friends or family to come up with a celebration of your own—something that honors an important event or season in your relationship with God. Make it a shared meal or a time of worship—whatever fits the content of the celebration. Then make a commitment to repeat that celebration annually, as just one more way to be reminded of God's goodness. You just can't have enough reminders of that.

Seeking Help

15. Write a prayer below (or simply pray one in silence), inviting God to work on your mind and heart in those areas you've noted in the Going Forward section. Be honest about your desires and fears.

Notes for Small Groups:

- *Look for ways to put into practice the things you wrote in the Going Forward section. Talk with other group members about your ideas and commit to being accountable to one another.*

- *During the coming week, ask the Holy Spirit to continue to reveal truth to you from what you've read and studied.*

- *Before you start the next lesson, read Leviticus 24—25. For more in-depth lesson preparation, read chapters 10 and 11, "Holy, Holy, Holy" and "This Land Is God's Land," in* Be Holy.

God's Land
(LEVITICUS 24—25)

Before you begin …
- *Pray for the Holy Spirit to reveal truth and wisdom as you go through this lesson.*
- *Read Leviticus 24—25. This lesson references chapters 10 and 11 in* Be Holy. *It will be helpful for you to have your Bible and a copy of the commentary available as you work through this lesson.*

Getting Started

From the Commentary

The most important structure in the camp of Israel was the tabernacle, the sanctuary where God dwelt and where the priests and Levites served Him. The outer covering of badgers' skins was not impressive, but within the tent of meeting, it was beautiful, costly, and glorious. It was the tabernacle that made the camp holy and set it apart for God, just as the presence of the Holy Spirit within believers sets them apart from the world and makes them wholly God's (1 Cor. 6:19–20; 2 Cor. 6:14–18; Eph. 1:13–14).

In Leviticus 24, the Lord gave Moses instructions concerning three holy things: the holy oil for the lampstand (vv. 1–4), the holy bread for the table (vv. 5–9), and the holy name of the Lord, which all the people were to honor (vv. 10–23).

—*Be Holy*, page 137

1. Why did God choose to dwell in the tabernacle during this point in biblical history? Why not show up in other ways? How did the physical building give a sense of structure and purpose to God's relationship with His people?

More to Consider: Bible students generally agree that oil for anointing is a symbol of the Holy Spirit of God, who anoints God's people for service (2 Cor. 1:21; 1 John 2:27). How is the oil mentioned in Leviticus 24 different? Zechariah 4 connects oil for burning with the Holy Spirit. What does the tabernacle lampstand signify?

2. Choose one verse or phrase from Leviticus 24—25 that stands out to you. This could be something you're intrigued by, something that makes you uncomfortable, something that puzzles you, something that resonates with you, or just something you want to examine further. Write that here.

Going Deeper

From the Commentary

> The veil divided the tabernacle proper into two parts, the Holy Place and the Holy of Holies. In the Holy Place were three pieces of furniture: the golden altar of incense, the table of presence bread, and the golden lampstand. As the priest faced the incense altar, the table would be to his right and the lampstand to his left.
>
> Since there were no windows in the tabernacle, it was necessary to have light in the Holy Place so the priests could see as they ministered there. The golden lampstand provided that light. It was hammered out of pure gold and made into one piece with a central shaft and six branches; pure olive oil fueled the lamps on the branches (see Ex. 25:31–39; 27:20–21; 30:7–8; 37:17–24; 40:24–25).
>
> —*Be Holy*, pages 137–38

3. Why is the specific arrangement of the tabernacle recorded in Scripture? What does this teach us about God's care and plan for His people? How did God use the symbolism of light in the tabernacle?

From the Commentary

Not only were the people to bring the pure olive oil for the lamp, but also they were to bring the fine flour out of which twelve loaves of bread were baked each week. These were put on the golden table each Sabbath, and then the old bread was given to the priests to eat.

The size of these loaves is a mystery to us because the text doesn't state the measure used in the recipe. The Hebrew simply reads "of two-tenths it shall be," but two-tenths of what? The NIV says "using two-tenths of an ephah," which would be about four quarts of flour, but the word *ephah* isn't in the Hebrew text. That much flour would produce a very large loaf, and it's doubtful that twelve large loaves would all fit on the table. It's probable that the loaves were stacked on top of one another, making two stacks of six loaves, with a small container of frankincense on top of each stack.

These loaves were treated like a meal offering, complete with the frankincense (Lev. 2:1–11). On the Sabbath, when the loaves were replaced, the priest would take a "memorial portion" from a loaf, add the frankincense, and burn it on the altar along with the daily burnt offering. The priests could then eat the old loaves, but they had to do it in the Holy Place (24:9).

—*Be Holy*, pages 139–40

4. What did the bread symbolize? Why were there twelve loaves on the table? The loaves were called the "bread of the Presence" (Ex. 25:30). How did the bread remind the priests that God was there not only for them but for all the people?

From the Commentary

It may seem strange to us that the book of Leviticus is interrupted at 24:10 to tell about a blasphemer who was judged, but the narrative is an illustration, not an interruption. The basis for obedience to the law is the fear of the Lord, and people who blaspheme His holy name have no fear of God in their hearts.

Every Jew knew the third commandment: "You shall not take the name of the LORD your God in vain, for the LORD will not hold him guiltless who takes His name in vain" (Ex. 20:7 NKJV). So fearful were the Jews of breaking this commandment that they substituted the name "Adonai" for "Jehovah" when they read the Scriptures, thus never speaking God's name at all. To respect a name is to respect the person who bears that name, and our highest respect belongs to the Lord.

—*Be Holy*, page 141

5. Why was the name of God so revered? What did taking the name of the Lord in vain say about that person's spiritual relationship with God? How does this rule about God hold true today? What is the difference (if there is one) between the honor given to God's name in the time of Leviticus and the honor given to God's name in today's church?

From the Commentary

The focus in Leviticus 25 and 26 is on Israel *in their land*. In fact, the word *land* is used thirty-nine times in these two chapters. The Lord's statement in 25:2 ("When you enter the land I am going to give you," NIV) must have been a great encouragement to Moses, especially after Israel failed to claim their inheritance at Kadesh-Barnea and had to wander in the wilderness (Num. 13—14).

If the Israelites were to possess and enjoy their land, they had to recognize and respect some basic facts, the first of which was that *God owned the land* (Lev. 25:2, 23, 38) and had every right to dispose of it as He saw fit. *God also owned the people of Israel* (v. 55), because He had redeemed them from Egyptian bondage. Because they belonged to Him, all the Jews were to treat one another as brothers and sisters (vv. 25, 35–38) and not take advantage of one another when it came to personal debts or property claims.

—Be Holy, page 149

6. Review Leviticus 25:1–7. What was expected of the Jews relating to the land? How did God define His own role regarding the Jews and their land (v. 21)? What was the connection between the way the Jews cared for their land and their relationship with God?

From the Commentary

When we studied Leviticus 23, we noted that the Jewish calendar was based on a series of sevens. There were seven annual feasts, three of them in the seventh month, and the seventh day of the week was the Sabbath, a day of rest. Now we learn that the seventh year was to be a year of rest for the land, the people, and their animals.

During the Sabbath Year, the people were not to work the fields or have organized harvests, but were to take from the fields the food they needed as it grew of itself. The people, including the poor and the aliens, could gather from the fields and be God's guests (Ex. 23:10–12).

Not only did the land rest, but also the people and the farm animals rested. The men certainly took care of the routine tasks that keep buildings from falling down, but they were not to engage in the normal activities of an agricultural society, like plowing, sowing, and harvesting. This prohibition also included the servants and the animals, all of whom were given a year of rest from their normal duties.

—*Be Holy*, page 150

7. Why did God make rest such an important issue for His people? Where else in the Bible did God teach or model the value of rest? How well does today's church honor rest? How can we do a better job of respecting and honoring rest?

From the Commentary

> The word *jubilee* is used six times in Leviticus 25:8–17
> and literally means "to sound the trumpet." (The Hebrew
> word is *yobel*, which means "a ram's horn.") For the people
> of Israel, each new year opened with the blowing of the
> trumpets on the first day of the seventh month, and ten
> days later, the people celebrated the Day of Atonement
> by fasting, repenting, and offering the required sacrifices.
> But every fiftieth year, at the close of the celebration of
> the Day of Atonement, the horns were blown again to
> announce that the Year of Jubilee had begun.
>
> —*Be Holy*, page 152

8. What elements were involved in the Year of Jubilee (Lev. 25:8–55)? Why
would it take a lot of faith to celebrate the Year of Jubilee? How did this
year teach the Jews the value of trusting God?

More to Consider: During the Year of Jubilee, the people were forbidden to carry on their normal agricultural pursuits but had to live on whatever the land produced. This gave both them and the land an extra year of rest, since the previous year would have been a Sabbath Year. How did this force them to rely on the Lord?

From the Commentary

If a poor Jew had to sell himself or his property in order to stay alive, he didn't have to wait until the Year of Jubilee to regain either his property or his freedom. At any time, a kinsman who was willing and able to pay the price could redeem him or his land.

If the former owner of the land was too poor to redeem his land, then a near kinsman could do it for him. But if the former owner somehow acquired the necessary wealth, he could redeem it for himself. The price would depend, of course, on the number of years (harvests) until the Year of Jubilee. If the man had neither a willing kinsman nor the necessary wealth, he would have to wait until the Year of Jubilee to regain his property.

—*Be Holy*, page 155

9. Why were there so many property rules? How did the property rules teach the people about God? In what ways did this chapter in the Jews' lives prepare them for what was to come, not only in the short term, but much later, when Jesus began His ministry?

From the Commentary

It's unfortunate that the Jewish people didn't obey the laws given in Leviticus 25, for their selfishness and greed brought ruin to the land and their economic system. The prophets rebuked the rich for exploiting the poor and stealing their houses, lands, and even their children (Isa. 3:14–15; 10:1–3; Amos 2:6–7; 5:11). The local courts ignored God's decrees; the judges, enriched by bribes, passed down decisions that favored the wealthy and crushed the poor. But God heard the cries of the poor and one day brought terrible judgment to the people of Israel.

—*Be Holy*, pages 158–59

10. How might following the rules in Leviticus 25 have helped the Jews avoid the corruption that soon followed? In what ways were the circumstances of that later corruption similar to what we see in the world today? In addition to creating the rules and regulations listed in Leviticus, how does God reveal His concern about the resources He's given us?

Looking Inward

Take a moment to reflect on all that you've explored thus far in this study of Leviticus 24—25. Review your notes and answers and think about how each of these things matters in your life today.

Tips for Small Groups: To get the most out of this section, form pairs or trios and have group members take turns answering these questions. Be honest and as open as you can in this discussion, but most of all, be encouraging and supportive of others. Be sensitive to those who are going through particularly difficult times and don't press for people to speak if they're uncomfortable doing so.

11. Have you ever thought of church as the place where God lives? If so, what prompted that way of thinking? How is that similar to the reality of Old Testament times when God appeared only in the tabernacle? What are some ways you meet God in church that you don't meet Him in other places?

12. The name of God is revered in Old Testament history. How do you treat God's name or names in your daily faith life? What are some ways you

show reverence to God? How do you balance that with the opportunity for an intimate relationship with God?

13. How do you show honor and care for the resources God has given us? In what ways does caring for the poor reflect God's long-standing truth? How does caring for the earth and all its creatures mirror God's own care?

Going Forward

14. Think of one or two things that you have learned that you'd like to work on in the coming week. Remember that this is all about quality, not quantity. It's better to work on one specific area of life and do it well than to work on many and do poorly (or to be so overwhelmed that you simply don't try).

Do you want to take rest more seriously? Be specific. Go back through Leviticus 24—25 and put a star next to the phrase or verse that is most encouraging to you. Consider memorizing this verse.

Real-Life Application Ideas: God wants us to care for the poor and also for this planet He has created. This week, come up with at least three different ways to help the poor or the planet. Maybe you can volunteer at a soup kitchen. Perhaps you can collect trash from the side of a highway. Choose activities that will stretch you a bit—don't settle on the easiest things you can do. Then, as you labor in your care, thank God that you are His hands and feet in a world that desperately needs both.

Seeking Help

15. Write a prayer below (or simply pray one in silence), inviting God to work on your mind and heart in those areas you've noted in the Going Forward section. Be honest about your desires and fears.

Notes for Small Groups:

- *Look for ways to put into practice the things you wrote in the Going Forward section. Talk with other group members about your ideas and commit to being accountable to one another.*

- *During the coming week, ask the Holy Spirit to continue to reveal truth to you from what you've read and studied.*

- *Before you start the next lesson, read Leviticus 26—27. For more in-depth lesson preparation, read chapters 12 and 13, "The Big Word 'If'" and "Learning from Leviticus," in* Be Holy.

If
(LEVITICUS 26—27)

Before you begin …
- *Pray for the Holy Spirit to reveal truth and wisdom as you go through this lesson.*
- *Read Leviticus 26—27. This lesson references chapters 12 and 13 in* Be Holy. *It will be helpful for you to have your Bible and a copy of the commentary available as you work through this lesson.*

Getting Started

From the Commentary

The word *if* has been called one of the shortest and yet one of the most important words in the English language. Debating over what might have happened in world history *if* Wellington had lost at Waterloo or *if* Lee had won at Gettysburg is an exercise in futility.

When you leave the "ifs" out of Leviticus 26—27, you may miss the meaning, for "if" is used thirty-two times.

The history of Israel can't be fully understood apart from the "ifs" contained in God's covenant. When it comes to Jewish history, "if" is a very big word. Three "if" phrases in chapter 26 show us the importance of the word: "If you walk in My statutes" (v. 3 NKJV); "But if you do not obey Me" (v. 14 NKJV); "But if they confess their iniquity" (v. 40 NKJV). In our relationship to the Lord, "if" carries a lot of weight.

—*Be Holy*, page 163

1. How would you summarize the statutes and instructions God gave Israel in Leviticus 26—27? How do these illustrate the responsibilities that every Christian believer has to the Lord? What does this connection teach us about God's hand in history?

2. Choose one verse or phrase from Leviticus 26—27 that stands out to you. This could be something you're intrigued by, something that makes you uncomfortable, something that puzzles you, something that resonates with you, or just something you want to examine further. Write that here.

Going Deeper

From the Commentary

> In Leviticus 26, to obey God is to "walk in [His] statutes" (v. 3), but to disobey Him is to "walk contrary" to the Lord and despise His statutes (vv. 15, 21, 23–24, 27–28, 40–41). The word translated "contrary" means "a hostile meeting with the intention of fighting."
>
> If I'm walking one direction and God is walking another, I'm moving away from His presence, *and God isn't about to change His direction!* If I continue to walk contrary to Him, I'm going to have serious problems, for "can two walk together, except they be agreed?" (Amos 3:3). Moses gave his people four excellent reasons why they should obey the Lord.
>
> *—Be Holy*, pages 163–64

3. Review Leviticus 26:1–13. According to these verses, what are the reasons why people should obey the Lord? Why should we obey God simply because of who He is? How easy is it to obey Him for that reason, compared to obeying Him for what He does or what He has promised?

More to Consider: If an Old Testament Jew sacrificed a pig on the altar or scattered human bones in the tabernacle courtyard, he would have been guilty of the grossest violations of God's holy law. How are the sins Christians indulge in today just as serious? In what ways are our bodies the sanctuary of God? What does that mean, practically speaking? (See 1 Cor. 6:15–20; Eph. 4:17–32.)

From the Commentary

As children of God, we already have everything we need for "life and godliness" (2 Peter 1:3), because we now possess "every spiritual blessing in Christ" (Eph. 1:3 NIV). But to possess these blessings is one thing; to enjoy them is quite something else. As we trust God's promises and obey His commandments, we draw upon our spiritual inheritance and are able to walk successfully and serve effectively. Like the nation of Israel in Canaan, we have battles to fight and work to do, but as we walk in obedience to the Lord, He enables us to overcome the enemy, claim the land, and enjoy its blessings.

To begin with, God promised them *rain and fruitful harvests* (Lev. 26:3–5, 10). An agricultural nation, Israel depended on the "latter rain" in the spring and the "former rain" in the autumn to provide water for their crops and to meet their domestic needs. One reason Baal worship ensnared the Israelites is because Baal was the Canaanite storm god. If the Jews needed rain, they sometimes turned to Baal for help instead of turning to Jehovah. If God wanted to discipline His people, He would often withhold the rain, as He did in the days of Elijah (1 Kings 17—18).

The Lord also promised them *peace and safety in their land* (Lev. 26:5–8). They could go to bed without fear of either animals or enemies invading their land. If the enemy did invade, the Jewish armies would soon chase them out, and one Jewish soldier would be worth twenty to a hundred of the enemy soldiers! Other nations depended for safety on large armies and supplies of horses and chariots, but Israel's victory came through faith in the Lord and obedience to His Word. "Some trust in chariots, and some in horses: but we will remember the name of the LORD our God" (Ps. 20:7).

—Be Holy, pages 166–67

4. Why did God make promises to the Israelites about the land? What was it about property that resonated with the Israelites? How does God's promise to bless obedience play out in the lives of believers today? Does obedience guarantee material prosperity? Explain.

From Today's World

Some of the "prosperity gospel" (obey God and you will receive rewards on earth) preachers today like to claim the covenant blessings listed in Leviticus for the church but prefer to apply the judgments to somebody else. If this covenant applies to God's children today, then we should be experiencing the judgments whenever we disobey Him. However, experience shows us that many compromising believers are successful, healthy, and wealthy, while many of God's faithful children are going through trials and difficulties. (See Ps. 73.)

5. Why is the message of the prosperity gospel so appealing to some believers? What, apart from the missing judgments noted in the previous paragraph, makes this belief system suspect? What are "success preachers" missing in their understanding and application of this passage in Leviticus?

From the Commentary

"For whom the LORD loves He chastens, and scourges every son whom He receives" (Heb. 12:6 NKJV; see Prov. 3:11–12). Israel's special relationship to Jehovah brought with it the obligation to obey His voice and glorify His name. "You only have I known [chosen] of all the families of the earth: therefore I will punish you for all your

iniquities" (Amos 3:2). Privilege brings with it responsibility, and no nation has enjoyed more spiritual privileges
from the Lord than the nation of Israel.

—*Be Holy*, page 168

6. Review Leviticus 26:14–39. Summarize the key points of the chastisement
described in these verses. What message does this list of punishments give
to God's people? Are we a privileged people still today? If so, how does God
relate to His people differently today from what's recorded in this passage?

From the Commentary

Even in the worst situations, however, there is always hope,
for the Lord is "merciful and gracious, longsuffering, and
abundant in goodness and truth, keeping mercy for thousands, forgiving iniquity and transgression and sin" (Ex.
34:6–7). His covenant with His people never changes,
and if we confess our sins and repent, He will forgive and
restore (Lev. 26:40–42; 1 Kings 8:33–34; Neh. 9:2; 1 John
1:9). Whether in blessing, chastening, or forgiving, God
always keeps His covenant and is true to His Word.

—*Be Holy*, pages 170–71

7. What are some examples of God's punishment of His people? How does He show up in the midst of their suffering? How does God's chastening bring His people back to Him? What does this look like in today's church?

From the Commentary

The cause of Israel's rebellion was "uncircumcised hearts," that is, hearts that had never been changed by the Lord (Lev. 26:41). The Jews boasted that they were circumcised in body, but that wasn't enough to save them (Matt. 3:7–12). The mark on the body was the outward seal of the covenant, but it took more than that to change the heart (see Deut. 10:16; 30:6; Jer. 4:4; 9:25; Rom. 2:29).

When we disobey the Lord, the enemy accuses us and wants us to believe there's no hope because God is through with us (2 Cor. 2:1–11). "If we are faithless, he will remain faithful, for he cannot disown himself" (2 Tim. 2:13 NIV). King Solomon pointed out the promise of forgiveness when he dedicated the temple (1 Kings 8:31–53), and it was that promise that Jonah claimed when he repented of his sins (Jonah 2:7).

—*Be Holy*, page 171

8. What is some evidence of "uncircumcised hearts" in today's church? What are some of the ways we disobey God? How does the promise of forgiveness in 1 John 1:9 provide encouragement for God's people when they have sinned?

From the Commentary

It seems strange that this book should end with a chapter on vows rather than with an account of a special demonstration of God's glory and holiness. But our promises to God must be as inviolable as His covenant with us. "Do not be rash with your mouth, and let not your heart utter anything hastily before God" (Eccl. 5:2 NKJV). "It is a snare for a man to devote rashly something as holy, and afterward to reconsider his vows" (Prov. 20:25 NKJV).

The principle behind the regulations in this chapter is that of substituting money for something given in dedication to God, a person, an animal, or a piece of property, and giving that money to the priests for the upkeep of the sanctuary. The priest would evaluate the gift according to the rules laid down in this chapter. By giving money in exchange for the gift, the worshipper was "redeeming" the gift but still fulfilling the vow. These vows were strictly voluntary and were expressions of the worshipper's gratitude to God for His blessing.

—*Be Holy*, page 172

9. What do our promises to God reveal about our hearts? How are the vows about giving money in Leviticus 27 similar to and different from the precepts on giving that appear in the New Testament?

More to Consider: The major lesson of Leviticus 27 is that God expects us to keep our commitments to Him and be honest in all our dealings with Him. Read 1 Samuel 15:22. How does what Samuel said to King Saul exemplify this? How do we live out this truth today?

From the Commentary

Eight times in Scripture, God said, "Be holy, for I am holy." Since God's commandments are God's enablements, this commandment assures us that it's possible to live a holy life. What health is to the body, holiness is to the soul, and the Great Physician can give us the spiritual health and wholeness that we need.

God wanted His people Israel to be "an holy nation" (Ex. 19:6), and this high calling applies to Christians today (1 Peter 2:9). Whatever else the church may be known for today—buildings, budgets, crowds, busy schedules—it certainly isn't known for its holiness. *How many Christians do you know about whom you could honestly say, "He is a man of God" or "She is a woman of God"?* How many "Christian celebrities" qualify?

—*Be Holy*, page 179

10. In what ways did Israel fail to be a holy nation? How did that failure affect their nation? How did it affect the pagans? Why is it important to emphasize verbal witness and godly character and conduct in a life of faith? How does a holy life dispel darkness and repel decay?

Looking Inward

Take a moment to reflect on all that you've explored thus far in this study of Leviticus 26—27. Review your notes and answers and think about how each of these things matters in your life today.

Tips for Small Groups: To get the most out of this section, form pairs or trios and have group members take turns answering these questions. Be honest and as open as you can in this discussion, but most of all, be encouraging and supportive of others. Be sensitive to those who are going through particularly difficult times and don't press for people to speak if they're uncomfortable doing so.

11. What does obedience mean to you? Are you comfortable with the idea of obeying God? How do you know what God wants you to do? Where do you turn to find the answer to that question?

12. Have you ever been tempted to follow prosperity gospel teaching? What is it about this theology that's so appealing? Where does it fall short for you? Is it wrong to count on God to bless His people? Explain.

13. What are some of the promises you've made to God? How well have you kept those? What do those promises reveal about your heart?

Going Forward

14. Think of one or two things that you have learned that you'd like to work on in the coming week. Remember that this is all about quality, not quantity. It's better to work on one specific area of life and do it well than to work on many and do poorly (or to be so overwhelmed that you simply don't try).

Do you want to follow through on a particular promise in your life? Be specific. Go back through Leviticus 26—27 and put a star next to the phrase or verse that is most encouraging to you. Consider memorizing this verse.

Real-Life Application Ideas: Take time this week to reflect on the promises God has made to you and the promises you've made to God. Think about the practical applications of both. How does each of those promises play out in everyday life? Are you treating God's promises as expectations? As evidence of God's character? Are you committed to your own promises, or are you just paying lip service to them? Use this week to come to a reasonable understanding of the role of promises in your relationship with God.

Seeking Help

15. Write a prayer below (or simply pray one in silence), inviting God to work on your mind and heart in those areas you've noted in the Going Forward section. Be honest about your desires and fears.

Notes for Small Groups:
- *Look for ways to put into practice the things you wrote in the Going Forward section. Talk with other group members about your ideas and commit to being accountable to one another.*
- *During the coming week, ask the Holy Spirit to continue to reveal truth to you from what you've read and studied.*

Summary and Review

Notes for Small Groups: This session is a summary and review of this book. Because of that, it is shorter than the previous lessons. If you are using this in a small-group setting, consider combining this lesson with a time of fellowship or a shared meal.

Before you begin ...
- *Pray for the Holy Spirit to reveal truth and wisdom as you go through this lesson.*
- *Briefly review the notes you made in the previous sessions. You will refer back to previous sections throughout this bonus lesson.*

Looking Back

1. Over the past eight lessons, you've examined Leviticus. What expectations did you bring to this study? In what ways were those expectations met?

2. What is the most significant personal discovery you've made from this study?

3. What surprised you most about Leviticus? What, if anything, troubled you?

Progress Report

4. Take a few moments to review the Going Forward sections of the previous lessons. How would you rate your progress for each of the things you chose to work on? What adjustments, if any, do you need to make to continue on the path toward spiritual maturity?

5. In what ways have you grown closer to Christ during this study? Take a moment to celebrate those things. Then think of areas where you feel you still need to grow and note those here. Make plans to revisit this study in a few weeks to review your growing faith.

Things to Pray About

6. Leviticus is a book about holiness and obedience. As you reflect on these themes, consider how you can live a God-honoring life that practices what it means to be holy.

7. The messages in Leviticus include holiness, obedience, God's faithfulness, the sanctity of sex, and trusting God's wisdom. Spend time praying about each of these topics.

8. Whether you've been studying this in a small group or on your own, there are many other Christians working through the very same issues you discovered when examining Leviticus. Take time to pray for them, that God would reveal truth, that the Holy Spirit would guide you, and that each person might grow in spiritual maturity according to God's will.

A Blessing of Encouragement

Studying the Bible is one of the best ways to learn how to be more like Christ. Thanks for taking this step. In closing, let this blessing precede you and follow you into the next week while you continue to marinate in God's Word:

May God light your path to greater understanding as you review the truths found in Leviticus and consider how they can help you grow closer to Christ.

The "BE" series . . .

For years pastors and lay leaders have embraced Warren W. Wiersbe's very accessible commentary of the Bible through the individual "BE" series. Through the work of David C Cook Global Mission, the "BE" series is part of a library of books made available to indigenous Christian workers. These are men and women who are called by God to grow the kingdom through their work with the local church worldwide. Here are a few of their remarks as to how Dr. Wiersbe's writings have benefited their ministry.

"Most Christian books I see are priced too high for me . . . I received a collection that included 12 Wiersbe commentaries a few months ago and I have read every one of them. I use them for my personal devotions every day and they are incredibly helpful for preparing sermons. The contribution David C Cook is making to the church in India is amazing."

—Pastor E. M. Abraham, Hyderabad, India

not just for North American readers!

"Resources in China are insufficient. I found this 'BE' series was very good for equipping and preaching . . .
We welcome more copies so that I can distribute them to all coworkers in the county in our annual training."
—Rev. Wang, Central China

To learn more about David C Cook Global Mission visit:
www.davidccook.org/global

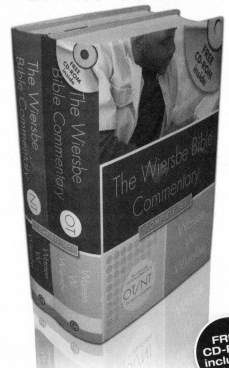